QUALITY–

Higher Education's
Principal Challenge

QUALITY—
Higher Education's Principal Challenge

Edited by
Thomas M. Stauffer

AMERICAN COUNCIL ON EDUCATION
Washington, D.C.

© 1981 by American Council on Education
    One Dupont Circle, Washington, D.C. 20036

Library of Congress Cataloging in Publication Data
Main entry under title:

Quality—higher education's principal challenge.

    1. Education, Higher—United States—Addresses,
essays, lectures. I. Stauffer, Thomas M. II. American Council on Education.
LA227.3.Q35   378.73   80-22366
ISBN 0-8268-1413-1

9 8 7 6 5 4 3 2 1

PRINTED IN THE UNITED STATES OF AMERICA

Contributors

Robert Arns
VICE PRESIDENT FOR ACADEMIC AFFAIRS, UNIVERSITY OF VERMONT

Jane Browning
ASSISTANT VICE PRESIDENT FOR RESEARCH AND DEVELOPMENT,
ATLANTA UNIVERSITY

Carolyne K. Davis
ASSOCIATE VICE PRESIDENT FOR ACADEMIC AFFAIRS,
UNIVERSITY OF MICHIGAN—ANN ARBOR

Barbara Knowles Debs
PRESIDENT, MANHATTANVILLE COLLEGE

Paul C. Gianini, Jr.
PRESIDENT, SPOON RIVER COLLEGE

Leonard L. Haynes III
DIRECTOR, OFFICE FOR THE ADVANCEMENT OF PUBLIC NEGRO
COLLEGES, NATIONAL ASSOCIATION OF STATE UNIVERSITIES
AND LAND-GRANT COLLEGES

D. Bruce Johnstone
PRESIDENT, STATE UNIVERSITY COLLEGE AT BUFFALO

Joseph F. Kauffman
PROFESSOR OF EDUCATIONAL ADMINISTRATION,
UNIVERSITY OF WISCONSIN—MADISON

H. R. Kells
PROFESSOR OF HIGHER EDUCATION, RUTGERS UNIVERSITY

Robert Kirkwood
EXECUTIVE DIRECTOR, COMMISSION ON HIGHER EDUCATION,
MIDDLE STATES ASSOCIATION OF COLLEGES AND SCHOOLS

Thomas M. Law
PRESIDENT, VIRGINIA STATE UNIVERSITY

Jack Lindquist
SENIOR ASSOCIATE, INSTITUTE FOR ACADEMIC IMPROVEMENT,
MEMPHIS STATE UNIVERSITY, AND INDEPENDENT CONSULTANT

William F. Massy
VICE PRESIDENT OF BUSINESS AND FINANCE, AND PROFESSOR
OF BUSINESS ADMINISTRATION, STANFORD UNIVERSITY

Isaac H. Miller, Jr.
PRESIDENT, BENNETT COLLEGE

John W. Nason
CONSULTANT TO THE ASSOCIATION OF GOVERNING BOARDS
OF UNIVERSITIES AND COLLEGES

Robert M. O'Neil
PRESIDENT, UNIVERSITY OF WISCONSIN; FORMERLY VICE PRESIDENT,
BLOOMINGTON CAMPUS, INDIANA UNIVERSITY

Sherry H. Penney
ASSOCIATE PROVOST OF THE UNIVERSITY, YALE UNIVERSITY

Dorothy G. Petersen
CONSULTANT, COUNCIL ON POSTSECONDARY ACCREDITATION

Charles J. Ping
PRESIDENT, OHIO UNIVERSITY

Adele Simmons
PRESIDENT, HAMPSHIRE COLLEGE

Lewis C. Solmon
PROFESSOR, GRADUATE SCHOOL OF EDUCATION, UNIVERSITY OF
CALIFORNIA, LOS ANGELES, AND SECRETARY-TREASURER,
HIGHER EDUCATION RESEARCH INSTITUTE

Thomas M. Stauffer
DIRECTOR, DIVISION OF EXTERNAL RELATIONS,
AMERICAN COUNCIL ON EDUCATION

Donald E. Walker
PRESIDENT, SOUTHEASTERN MASSACHUSETTS UNIVERSITY

Contents

Foreword

IN THE HIGHER EDUCATION COMMUNITY, our most precious asset is public confidence. If we are to keep that confidence, we must maintain quality in the academic and other missions which the public has entrusted to our enterprise. If we fail to do so, the public will, rightfully, withhold its support. The challenge to realize the highest possible standards is never ending, and it is also what makes an academic career worthwhile.

The challenge to maintain quality should not be interpreted as a sweeping plea to establish high admission standards and a ruthless grading system. Quality institutions are not confined to those with highly selective admissions, although quality may be easier to maintain in such institutions than in those whose mandate is to provide open educational opportunity. High quality may be found among open-admissions institutions, as inferior quality may be found among highly selective institutions.

Whether the mission is off-campus or on-campus instruction, a university without walls or one with an ivory tower, a two- or four-year program, a research or a teaching orientation or some combination thereof, secular or religious, the challenge to maintain quality is always before us.

A review of articles in this book suggests that the challenge has never been so great. Formidable complexities and forces beyond the control of the higher education enterprise seem ready to undermine quality. My greatest worry is that academic leaders, administrators, faculty members, and trustees alike will become discouraged by the bad news, so readily available, and overlook the opportunities and even the good news about higher education's future. Low morale may not be unrealistic, but we must guard against a paralysis of fear.

The articles deal with questions of quality in a constructive spirit. That approach is both pragmatic and wise, I think. Higher education at the end of the 1980s will have unfulfilled agenda, like the substantial ones remaining at the end of the 1970s and 1960s. I suspect that the decade will prove neither as bad nor as good as some predict, but I am confident that much now on the higher education agenda will have been accomplished. A positive, realistic outlook will go far in promoting realization of our goals for quality, access, and public service.

To this end, the American Council on Education commissioned articles about quality for its 1979 annual meeting. Selections from these papers are included in this volume. The constructive tone from the contributors signals the Council's own orientation toward academic quality: illuminating the problems, setting practical solutions or directions, and providing leadership. The academic community can expect the American Council to pursue maintenance of educational quality as a highest priority. This volume marks an important contribution toward this end.

J. W. PELTASON, *President*
American Council on Education

Acknowledgments

ARTICLES INCLUDED IN THIS VOLUME were commissioned as background papers for forums convened in Houston, Texas, at the 1979 annual meeting of the American Council on Education. Forum leaders, represented in this volume, were invited to address topics and engage in discussions with the audience, elaborating ideas developed in the papers. The papers were neither read nor distributed in Houston.

The American Council on Education is grateful to all who participated in these forums, audience and forum leaders alike. Papers revised after the meeting frequently reflect ideas developed in the forum discussions. In addition, I am indebted to a hundred-member annual meeting design committee, members of the Council's staff, and members of the Washington Higher Education Secretariat who made recommendations about topics and forum leaders included in this volume. It was evident that the number of topics and persons qualified to write on them was far greater than could be included here.

Finally, I happily acknowledge the good and capable work of the ACE Publications Department, directed by Marcy V. Massengale. In particular, careful editing by Olive Mills has greatly strengthened this volume, very much in the tradition of her long career as senior editor of the American Council on Education. Her service was highlighted at the 1979 Houston meeting's annual banquet by Council President J. W. Peltason, who made an award and read the following statement:

> OLIVE MILLS, senior editor of the Publications Department; defender of the written word against barbarians foreign and domestic; challenger of the inane, the trite, the puffed-up, enemy of plural learnings and singular criteria; physician of the flabby phrase, surgeon of the swollen sentence, dermatologist of the disfigured paragraph, dentist for prose without bite, and midwife for our unborn thoughts. We humbly acknowledge that the Council's authority, forcefulness, and grace in print over thirty-five years have rested squarely on your knowledge, care, faithfulness, good sense, good cheer, and diplomacy. In partial payment for the debts we owe you, we pledge to maintain the standards you have set for the staff as writers and for the Council as publisher.

Her colleagues on the Council staff and contributors to this volume, I am sure, happily acknowledge the accuracy of President Peltason's statement.

THOMAS M. STAUFFER

Quality in American Higher Education

THOMAS M. STAUFFER

QUALITY IN AMERICAN HIGHER EDUCATION—what it is, how to measure it, and how to promote and certify it—is an enduring concern among educators and the public alike. Two hundred years ago Governor Thomas Jefferson of Virginia proposed to upgrade the curriculum at the College of William and Mary along new Revolutionary lines. Although his proposals were not fully enacted by the legislature, his initiative helped legitimate shaping a pattern for higher education in the United States for which European standards of quality were not entirely applicable.

By the late nineteenth and early twentieth centuries, associations of academic leaders were being formed, the College Entrance Examination Board was founded, and conferences were held—notable was the 1906 meeting in Williamstown, Massachusetts, from which the American pattern of accreditation evolved—with the specified purpose of improving quality standards. In 1924 and 1934, President Raymond Hughes of Miami University (Ohio) and later of Iowa State conducted the first studies to rate quality in graduate programs. Abraham Flexner's famous 1910 report on medical schools forced those of the lowest quality out of business.

Today, the debate is at a high pitch and, arguably, is more important than ever before. In 1900, college enrollments were roughly a quarter million, from a population base of 76 million; now, almost 12 million students are enrolled in accredited nonprofit institutions on a population base of about 225 million. The latter enrollment figure does not count millions more enrolled in postsecondary education programs of business concerns and other entities. The sheer proportion of the population involved in higher education is but one indication of the national influence that colleges and universities carry through their teaching, research, and general service. As a result, the quality of the product is getting a closer look.

Quality of the American way of life, of the nation's institutions, and of the economy are now staples of American political debate. Values previ-

1

ously unquestioned have been examined, sometimes to the point of exhaustion under the combined weight of the civil rights movement, the Vietnam war, Watergate, inflation, and the energy crisis. Higher education has not been immune. State boards of higher education, made enormously stronger in the 1970s, have moved into areas of curriculum quality control, although primary responsibility for academic programs is still acknowledged to rest with faculty members. Federal government intrusion, through all three branches, into institutions has had a similar effect. Academics themselves have inquired how they should be held "accountable" to the public's trust. By mid-1980, roughly 4,500 postsecondary institutions were accredited by some fifty voluntary agencies.[1] But the status of academic accreditation itself has come under sharp criticism. Some off-campus and nontraditional programs have often proved difficult to evaluate, and their quality has often been attacked.

In addition to academic quality, the quality of practices and procedures has been scrutinized as never before. Here, outside agencies are involved. Practices and procedures that draw particular attention include employment conditions, labor union organizations, financial and resource reporting, athletics, real or potential discrimination, admissions and marketing policies, and ethical standards. One consequence of this attention has been the move by higher education associations to develop self-regulation guidelines for colleges and universities. Either from an interest in ethics or the threat of regulation by government agencies, institutions, by applying these general guidelines to their individual situations, can get their own houses in order before external action is brought to bear.

But quality assessment, whether academic or procedural, is inherently difficult. There are no agreed-upon, defined standards for measurement, let alone methods for improving them. The late Allan M. Cartter neatly summarized the dilemma, "Quality is someone's subjective assessment, for there is no way of objectively measuring what is in essence an attribute of value."[2]

Normativeness is inherent in quality control and appears unlikely to diminish. Even when definitions and methodology are designed with precision, controversy ensues: attempts in the last several decades to assess the quality of graduate programs are a case in point. As already noted,

1. Sherry S. Harris, ed., *1980–81 Accredited Institutions of Postsecondary Education* (Washington: American Council on Education, 1980).

2. *An Assessment of Quality in Graduate Education* (Washington: American Council on Education, 1966), p. 4.

Hughes conducted the first studies, in 1924 for the Association of American Colleges and in 1934 for the American Council on Education (ACE). The work developed from his interest in offering his students some guidance in choosing appropriate graduate schools. Parenthetically, one justification for creating the Association of American Universities in 1900 was the felt need to certify to European universities which American institutions educated students at quality levels meriting admission to their doctoral programs. Other evaluative studies were made, by Hayward Keniston of the University of Pennsylvania in 1957, and by Allan Cartter in 1966 and, later, by Kenneth D. Roose and Charles J. Andersen for ACE. In addition, *Change* magazine and other journals have published evaluations of professional schools, and federal agencies have made evaluations of their own. Always, the evaluations have touched off controversy, both on technical details and on their use or, rather, misuse. The Roose-Anderson study, despite caveats in their book, was often used as a simple ranking without regard for a multitude of subtleties.[3] Whatever the controversies, there still must be something compelling about such evaluations. After several years of debate, the National Research Council, under the auspices of the Conference Board of Associated Research Councils, consisting of the four major academic coordinating bodies, is planning a study which, it is said, will take into account many problems associated with past assessments.

Two other matters are drawing controversy: the ability to maintain quality in mass higher education and the influence of institutional quality on students. Nisbet has argued that the American obsession with equal opportunity has lowered overall quality,[4] whereas Howard Bowen appears unconvinced. His evidence points to the "significant positive effects of higher education on both individuals and society," such that "higher education, taken as a whole, is enormously effective" and "well worth what it costs."[5] Higher education, he believes, does contribute to overall expansion of intellectual capacities and to the quality of social and national life. Most students of this problem usually find refuge in the many categories of institutions available to students, from highly selective to open-door admissions, American higher education being sufficiently diverse to ac-

3. Roose and Andersen, *A Rating of Graduate Programs* (Washington: American Council on Education, 1970), pp. 1–2.

4. Robert Nisbet, *The Degradation of the Academic Dogma* (New York: Basic Books, 1971).

5. Howard Bowen, *Investment in Learning* (San Francisco: Jossey-Bass, 1977), pp. 431–32, 448.

commodate a multiplicity of interests and talents. Astin and Panos, however, suggest that this view may be an exaggeration. The characteristics which students bring to their college or university, they argue, outweigh institutional influence.[6] Solmon and Taubman demur, though, in their findings that "the quality of institution [has] impact on the lifetime earnings of students."[7]

Translating these findings, whichever ones are chosen, into operational policies is no easy task. Academic administrators, trustees, and faculty leaders seek guidance, but the move from data and opinion to practice involves controversy over institutional priorities and willingness to act. Findings about quality, even if campus leaders have the time and background to evaluate them, may be inadequate for use at a specific institution. Astin argues, for example, that these leaders lack feedback on the educational condition of their institutions in the way that feedback is available to managers in corporations and government agencies on their work. Often colleges and universities are bound by financial models that stress resource manipulation rather than data on quality. He reports that his research findings demonstrate the importance of student development data in ascertaining the condition of institutional quality, especially data on the use of student time. Such data are routinely ignored in favor of resource data, a priority which trustees and administrators feel they must emphasize for reporting and managerial purposes.[8]

Ashworth argues that gauging quality goes beyond institutional priorities to national priorities and a willingness of educational leaders to act on evidence of declining quality.[9] Ashworth, Texas commissioner of higher education, has developed a cyclical theory of quality ebb and flow in American higher education. In the later stages of expansion, successively after the Morrill Act of 1862, the GI Bill at the end of World War II, and Sputnik in 1957, shoddy education and poor quality and practice became commonplace. The current low state can be rectified only if national leaders, especially academicians, are willing to make the necessarily tough

6. Alexander W. Astin and Robert Panos, *The Educational and Vocational Development of College Students* (Washington: American Council on Education, 1969), pp. 130–32, 145.

7. Lewis C. Solmon and Paul J. Taubman, *Does College Matter?* (New York: Academic Press, 1973), p. 3.

8. Alexander W. Astin, "Student-Oriented Management: A Proposal for Change," in *Evaluating Educational Quality: A Conference Summary* (Washington: Council on Postsecondary Accreditation, 1979), pp. 3–18.

9. Kenneth H. Ashworth, *American Higher Education in Decline* (College Station: Texas A&M University Press, 1979).

decisions to improve matters, he argues. Ashworth's targets in particular are nontraditional programs, accreditation practices, and educators willing to put up with low quality.

Many academic leaders believe that academic quality and procedural quality will exceed other factors in determining, not simply the prosperity of the institutions, but how important a role colleges and universities will play in American life through the end of this century. The American Council on Education, in deciding to explore issues raised by Astin, Nisbet, and the others[10] and by commissioning the articles that follow, emphasized articulation between data and values, on one hand, and policies and practices on the other. The model policies, exemplary programs, and telling analyses and suggestions presented should stimulate and aid campus leaders in confronting problems they face.

Although, by definition, only a few institutions can be of highest quality, all academicians have the professional responsibility to strive continuously for excellence. With the integrity of American colleges and universities under close scrutiny and even attack, the necessity of this obligation is underscored. As a corollary and example: when the United States position in world technology is under challenge, the national consequences of inattention to quality are obvious. The American Council on Education, through this volume and by other means, plans to remain active and visible in encouraging realization of this goal.

10. Thomas M. Stauffer, "Competition and Quality," *Educational Record*, Summer 1979, pp. 225–26.

1. QUALITY IN HIGHER EDUCATION— WHAT IS IT?

A Multidimensional Approach to Quality

LEWIS C. SOLMON

THE DICTIONARY defines "quality" as (1) "character with respect to excellence, fineness, or grade of excellence; (2) high grade, superior excellence [in] an accomplishment or attainment; and (3) character or nature, as belonging to or distinguishing a thing" (*Random House Dictionary of the English Language*). In applying these definitions to "quality" in higher education, the key words seem to be "excellence," "accomplishment," and "distinguishing." Yet these three concepts may be quite different. "Distinguishing" may refer to institutions that, by being leaders or innovators, are different. "Accomplishment" may refer to institutions that achieve and hence affect various participants in the educational process. Finally, "excellence" probably comes closest to connoting what is usually viewed as quality in higher education—a consensus that an institution or a program is superior. The unresolved question is, How is this superiority measured, that is, superiority along what dimensions? And superiority compared to what?

Recently, a researcher at the Higher Education Research Institute found a quotation in *Zen and the Art of Motorcycle Maintenance* that perhaps summarizes the problem of getting at the concept of concern here:

> Quality . . . you know what it is, yet you don't know what it is. But that's self-contradictory. But some things are better than others, that is, they have more quality. But when you try to say what that quality is, apart from the things that have it, it all goes poof! There's nothing to talk about. But if you can't say what quality is, how do you know that it even exists? If no one knows what it is, then for all practical purposes it doesn't exist at all. But for all practical purposes it does exist. What else are the grades based on? Why else would people pay fortunes for some things and throw others in the trash pile? Obviously some things are better than others . . . but what's the 'betterness'. . . . So round and round you go, spinning mental wheels and nowhere finding anyplace to get traction. What the hell is Quality? What is it?[1]

---

1. Robert Pirsig (New York: Bantam, 1975), p. 178.

Perhaps by posing and answering two related questions, we may throw light on the question, Quality in higher education—what is it?

First, in what context has quality in higher education been dealt with?

Simplistic notions of quality have been developed for use in the accrediting process. In order to make certain that institutions and their programs are worthy of their clientele and of the resources that accrue to them, professional associations and regional accrediting groups periodically conduct reviews to determine whether institutions or programs are to be, or should remain, accredited. The presumption is that accredited institutions and programs are of higher quality than nonaccredited ones.[2] Hence, the evaluation more closely resembles a "pass-fail" system than a system of grades: certain minimum standards are required, but no differentiations or comparisons are made among those that pass or among those that fail.

Usually, a requirement for accreditation is that institutional or program goals be clear (probably so that students can look for a match with their own goals), and at times some evaluation of the institution's ability to achieve these goals is conducted. In general, the accreditation evaluation accepts at face value a correspondence between resource availability and the likelihood of achieving goals.[3] (This brief summary ignores the sometimes substantial differences between the process of regional accrediting bodies and that of professional associations.) The process has become that of rating quality according to resources available but neglecting to test the relationships between resources and goal achievement. Hence, the counting of library books, faculty members with doctorates, and students per classroom has been part of quality assessments, while alumni achievements and students' satisfaction with their educational experience have not. Perhaps the most indictable aspect of the accreditation approach to quality is the generally uncritical acceptance of the stated goals, that is, the failure to determine whether institutional or program objectives warrant support—regardless of whether the goals are achieved. For example, if a college aims to increase student satisfaction by emphasizing athletics to

2. William K. Selden, *Accreditation and the Public Interest* (Washington: Council on Postsecondary Accreditation, 1977), and Kenneth E. Young, "Accreditation and Graduate Education," in *Proceedings of the Sixteenth Annual Meeting of the Council of Graduate Schools in the United States,* Denver, December 8–10, 1976 (Washington: The Council, 1977), pp. 133–38.

3. William E. Troutt, "Regional Accreditation Evaluative Criteria and Quality Assurance," *Journal of Higher Education,* March–April 1979, pp. 199–210.

the detriment of the academic program, is this an appropriate approach even if it succeeds?

The Rating Game

The other extreme in the assessment of institutional or program quality seems to have developed from the American interest in excellence per se and in competition.[4] Just as Americans are interested in the top ten movies of all time, in the largest corporations in any year, and so on, we are interested in knowing which are the best colleges, the best graduate programs in economics. And those in the institutions of higher learning are also interested in knowing where they rate, less as a guide to how to do better than as a discussion topic over cocktails.

And, just as many people find the evaluations of television programs by Nielsen families less interesting than the evaluations by *New York Times* or *T.V. Guide* reviewers, so the surveys of "experts" have gained most attention among academics. An expert, by definition, need not explain why he prefers A to B; what is of most interest is which he prefers. The academic analogue to the Nielsen families' ratings would be the popularity of various colleges among able college applicants—the so-called selectivity measure.[5] Of course, in both cases, the preferences of the "consumers" are significantly influenced by the experts' reviews. Hence, in academe, as in the performing arts, colleges and their programs have been reviewed periodically—by experts. But unlike movie reviews, the reviews of quality in academe have occurred only infrequently and their effects linger. And because more movies and colleges receive negative rather than positive reviews, those "in the business" generally exhibit a strong dislike for ratings and the raters, inasmuch as the majority of movies and of universities do not find themselves among the year's "top ten."

Quality ratings in higher education are criticized for halo effects, reputation lags, biases built in by institutional size and age, and more. They are said to be more subjective than scientific, to reward large, orthodox research institutions, and to deny recognition for diversity, innovation, and nontraditional models. They lend themselves too easily to quantitative and ordinal interpretations when perhaps, some argue, many institutions are meritorious even though not highly ranked.[6]

4. M. J. Clark, "The Meaning of Quality in Graduate and Professional Education," in *Scholars in the Making: The Development of Professional Students*, ed. Joseph Katz and Rodney T. Hartnett (Cambridge, Mass.: Ballinger, 1976), pp. 85–104.

5. Alexander W. Astin, *Four Critical Years* (San Francisco: Jossey-Bass, 1977).

6. W. P. Dolan, *The Ranking Game* (Lincoln: University of Nebraska, 1976).

Since most education associations represent more institutions *not* in the top ten than in the top ten, they oppose subjective reputation ratings with vigor. Yet two points must be made in rebuttal. First, the subjective ratings based on expert opinions are almost always highly correlated with any measure of objective criteria that can reasonably be assumed to be related to process measures of "quality" or "excellence," but not necessarily with value-added measures.[7] More important, in the absence of periodic reassessments, the hierarchy will ossify, and institutions that deserve to have their positions changed (either for better or worse) will not be reevaluated.

The Changing Functions of "Quality"

The pros and cons of ratings lead to the second question which might guide an understanding of quality *Why should quality or excellence be a concern?*

Higher education is, for diverse reasons, facing a period of retrenchment after decades of growth. The economic situation in the country has changed. Demographics dictate that there will be fewer people in the traditional college-age cohort. And the value of advanced education is being reassessed nationally, in part because the favored position of the college-educated in the labor market has inevitably been reduced as the proportion of the population with college degrees has increased.

As a result, potential students are spending time deciding *whether or not* to go to college, but, in many instances, are even more concerned about *where* to go. When the degree itself no longer serves as an indicator of a worthy employee, and when grades are less valid because of grade inflation, the quality of the degree becomes even more vital. Hence, a college whose ranking falls may be seriously hurt by the lower numbers and lower quality in its applicant pool.

Additionally, many states, along with the federal government, are becoming increasingly concerned with the efficient allocation of scarce resources, and it is only logical that high quality programs and institutions will be judged to deserve the most support.[8] From the perspectives of both the students and the funders, however, traditional measures of quality

7. See, for example, M. J. Clark, R. T. Hartnett, and L. I. Baird, *Assessing Dimensions of Quality in Doctoral Education: A Technical Report of a National Study in Three Fields* (Princeton, N.J.: Educational Testing Service, 1976); David E. Drew, *Science Development: An Evaluation Study* (Washington: National Academy of Science, 1975); and Charles F. Elton and S. A. Rogers, "The Departmental Rating Game: Measure of Quantity or Quality?" *Higher Education* 2 (1973): 439–46.

8. R. J. Barak and Robert O. Berdahl, *State-level Academic Program Review in Higher Education* (Denver, Colo.: Education Commission of the States, 1978).

may be inappropriate. Although Harvard might be higher ranked than Los Angeles Community College, all students cannot fit into Harvard, and even some who could might benefit more from the two-year college's program. If only the traditionally highly rated programs are supported, the funding agency seeking to use postsecondary education as a vehicle for increasing educational opportunity and socioeconomic mobility might be putting its money in the wrong place.

The point is that as the functions of postsecondary education change from those associated with a meritocracy, and with a training ground for the best and the brightest, to those associated with a vehicle for upward social mobility and expanded access for adults, women, and minorities, then assessments of excellence in the traditional sense must give way to assessments of quality measured by "distinctiveness" and "accomplishment" along a multitude of dimensions. It seems that survival alone in these trying times for education implies high quality in one way or another. And, we must hope, the resistance by the higher education establishment is more advocacy of new criteria for, rather than an opposition to, evaluation of the success of universities and colleges in achieving a multitude of worthy goals. To reject diversity—of institutions and of goals—is to resist providing the consumers and funders of higher education with any description of the system at all.

Too often, institutional or departmental quality is described by an aggregate measure where each educational unit's worth is compared to all units in the country, regardless of their diverse goals. The two evaluative techniques most frequently employed are ratings of experts and accumulations of seemingly more objective (measurable) data on characteristics of the institutions or departments (including their students, faculty, and resources)—data assumed to be associated with the amorphous concept of quality. Although the latter kinds of data are generally viewed as less subject to raters' personal tastes, even these are subjective assessments of what the dimensions of quality are or should be.

Suggestions for Broader Criteria

The concept of quality must be broadened by reviewing efforts already made, by providing new data for illustrative purposes, and by emphasizing the following points:

1. Quality assessments must take into account institutional or departmental goals, evaluate the desirability of these goals from a variety of

perspectives, and determine the extent to which goals are achieved. Such assessments may be viewed in part as the accreditation perspective.[9]

2. An important component in assessing the achievement of desirable goals is the "value added" approach. That is, educational outputs considered in a vacuum are inadequate measures of quality because inputs have not been controlled. This approach has been advocated by a number of researchers including this author.[10]

3. Depending on the constituencies to be served by different institutions or departments, institutions that accomplish very different things may be of equally high quality. Therefore, a variety of quality measures are required and national comparisons on aggregate scales are quite useless. The latter reflect traditional state concerns.[11]

4. In particular, distinctions must be made between national research universities and the colleges and universities that are satisfying a variety of regional and local needs. The interest in research and training has always been a high national priority.

5. Other dimensions of quality include student satisfaction, access and retention, achievements of alumni, available resources, faculty and administrator satisfaction and achievements, services provided to local and broader communities, innovativeness and leadership in developing new approaches for achieving goals, and rates of improvement in each of these dimensions. Given institutional missions and context, these goals are of varying importance.[12]

Hence, we must answer the question "What is quality?" by suggesting new criteria. The recent pilot study made by the Council of Graduate Schools and the Educational Testing Service advocates multiple indicators which can be used primarily for self-assessment and institutional improvement, indicators concerned with educational procedures and academic climate. These might not correlate with research-related variables that have been found to be highly related to peer reputation ratings. That is, measures of student satisfaction (during college, immediately afterward, and several years later—and these might differ), teaching and the learning environment, faculty interaction, and the like must be considered and perhaps given more weight than peer review.

9. Kenneth E. Young, "Evaluating Institutional Effectiveness," *Educational Record*, Winter 1976, pp. 45–52.

10. Astin, *Four Critical Years;* Lewis C. Solmon, "The Definition of College Quality and Its Impact on Earnings," *Explorations in Economic Research*, Fall 1975, pp. 537–87.

11. Barak and Berdahl, *State-level Academic Program Review*.

12. Clark, Hartnett, and Baird, *Assessing Dimensions of Quality in Doctoral Education*.

Even the concept of leadership must be reconsidered. The highly rated institutions[13] are still viewed as having great national influence—an abstract term. But very different schools, namely, those of the same type and in geographical proximity, are viewed in a recent study to be the most innovative or to influence local institutions most strongly.[14]

Overall, a number of points must be stressed:

- Different types of institutions (particularly specialty institutions like Juilliard) and different types of programs must be judged on criteria appropriate to their respective types. Special efforts must be made to identify special strengths and weaknesses of every institution.
- Quality assessments must extend beyond the leading twenty or thirty institutions, regardless of the criteria used. Too often those not at the top are viewed as failures; this blanket presumption is wrong and harmful.
- Consumerism must be taken into account with the following caveats. Colleges should seek to satisfy their clients, but not to the extent of spraying laughing gas over the campus. Student priorities and values should be considered to the extent that they are consistent with educational goals. Conversely, exclusive reliance on student satisfaction measures might be harmful.
- The potential value of employers and practicing professionals (who are also clients and consumers) as evaluators should be considered. Who knows more about the quality of a law school's training than lawyers?
- Quality should no longer be confused with quantity. "Large" need not be better, and we must resist the temptation to evaluate only what can easily be measured.
- "Value added," as a concept, should be brought to the fore in quality assessments. After controlling for what students bring with them to a program, particularly native ability, we must try to assess what the student gets out of college, how much he or she has grown beyond normal maturation. This element is particularly important when access is expanded to less able students.
- In using any kind of student outcomes, it is also useful (perhaps critical) to distinguish between the effects of the education (value added) and

13. For example, Allan M. Cartter, *An Assessment of Quality in Graduate Education* (Washington: American Council on Education, 1966), and Kenneth D. Roose and Charles J. Andersen, *A Rating of Graduate Programs* (Washington: American Council on Education, 1970).

14. Richard R. Johnson, "Leadership Among American Colleges," *Change*, November 1978, pp. 50–51.

educational credentialing (screening and sorting). Too often we tend to equate the two functions.

- We must identify the institution's or the program's contributions not only to the student, but also to the community and to the general social well-being—contributions that are at times almost impossible to quantify or evaluate.
- We must always do dynamic rather than static evaluations, that is, consider not only where an institution is, but also where it has come from and what its potential for improvement is.
- Perhaps one overall conclusion is that it is all right to assess quality by asking people their opinions—even if those polled cannot define "quality." But others besides a few experts must be polled—students, employers, families, the public must be included. And what is being evaluated must be explicated (for example, learning environment, reputation, community service, role in increasing access, value added to student competences) even if the criteria for assessment are not.

The views expressed here may be summarized by quoting Allan Cartter's prophetic study from the mid 1960s.

> Diversity can be a costly luxury if it is accomplished by ignorance. Our present system works fairly well because most students, parents, and prospective employers know that a bachelor's degree from Harvard, Stanford, Swarthmore, or Reed is ordinarily a better indication of ability and accomplishment than a bachelor's degree from Melrose A&M or Siwash College. Even if no formal studies were ever undertaken, there is always a grapevine at work to supply impressionistic evaluations. However, evaluation by rumor and word of mouth is far from satisfactory, particularly in advanced training for scholarship and the professions. In stating the case for studies of quality at the undergraduate level, David Riesman has argued:
>
> "The quality of a school changes faster than its clientele recognizes; and colleges that have developed a novel or more demanding program cannot get the students to match it, while other institutions that have decayed cannot keep away students who should no longer go there. While autos carry their advertising, so to speak, on their body shells, which speak as loudly as print or TV commercials, colleges can change inside their shells with hardly anyone's noticing. And the result can be tragic, not only for misled students, but for imaginative faculty and administrators who may not live long enough to be rewarded by the appearance of good students attracted by those changes."
>
> Just as consumer knowledge and honest advertising are requisite if a competitive economy is to work satisfactorily, so an improved knowledge of opportunities and of quality is desirable if a diverse educational system is to work effectively—especially under retrenchment.
>
> Evaluation of quality in education, at both the undergraduate and graduate

levels, is important not only in determining the front-ranking institutions, but also in identifying lower-ranking colleges. Many prospective graduate students would not be suited to an education at Harvard, the Rockefeller Institute, or California Institute of Technology. Other institutions, in view of their educational offerings, level of work, and quality of students, would provide a happier and more productive experience. Universities, through their selection procedures, and students, through their natural proclivities, tend to sort themselves out into congenial environments.[15]

Cartter has left us with a challenge to which we have only begun to respond adequately.

Quality Education Is Lifelong Development for Each

JACK LINDQUIST

LET'S START WITH A SIMPLE PREMISE. Education should be judged on its capacity to facilitate the lifelong intellectual, ethical, and personal-career development of each student accepted into its institutions. A high quality education is education that enables each of its students to proceed to higher development in life. And while "higher" has obvious socioeconomic connotations, education should aid students in going higher in the "higher" parts of Maslow's hierarchy of human needs—self- and social acceptance and esteem as well as the sophisticated pursuit of truth, beauty, and justice.[1]

This premise includes three critical aspects, all of which are attracting more attention on the fringe of education than at its core. They are "lifelong," "development," and "each." Why should such words be at the heart of the next decade's definitions of quality in education?

Lifelong Education

"Terminal" education is encountering many problems these days. Educators have been saying for two decades that some kinds of knowledge become obsolete so quickly that to regard preparatory education as *the* final education is, at best, naïve. Yet the thrust of many educational programs remains knowledge acquisition rather than the skill of knowledge

15. Cartter, *An Assessment of Quality in Graduate Education*, p. 3; David Riesman, *Constraint and Variety in American Education* (New York: Doubleday, 1958), p. 5.

1. Abraham H. Maslow, *The Farther Reaches of Human Nature* (New York: Viking, 1972).

acquisition. We educators also know that interest in and concern for learning varies throughout life: what might be useless force-feeding to an eighteen-year-old may be a banquet to the same person twenty years later. I, for example, would like to learn more about ancient civilization now. At eighteen, I was mainly interested in my jump shot, my social life, and the modern novel. Yet few educational programs build curricula on the basis of sensitivity to the life cycle, or what Havighurst calls "developmental tasks." Instead we teach what we think the "educated man" [*sic*] should know, whether or not the timing is appropriate for the student. Finally, we educators know that in the next fifteen years the pool of eighteen-year-olds will decrease by a quarter to a half of its present size. There is nothing we can do now to make more 1970 births. So, whether or not we like the idea of educating adults, it is becoming our reality. We are forced to consider that formal assistance to learning might be a lifelong challenge.

What does recent attention to lifelong education have to do with quality? Rapidly obsolescing knowledge and skill are not high quality in the long run. They must be renewed. A school might stake its reputation on excellent preparation at one phase of a student's personal and professional life. But that phase is quickly past. The student may have received a terrific Harvard pre-med education in the late seventies, but much of the knowledge may be out of date by the late eighties. If that person a decade after Harvard is not still attempting to be on top of medical knowledge, patients are in trouble, Harvard graduate or not. A high quality education, therefore, is one that returns in the form of continuing renewal. A high quality school helps students develop not just current expertise but also the desire and skill to keep abreast.

A word here about enthusiasm for learning. For a four-year-old, learning, even formal education (nursery school), can be fun. Although the child has not acquired what Whitehead notes as the necessary complement to the romance of learning—painstaking diligence,[2] the educational challenge is not to replace romantic curiosity with drudgery. The task is to maintain the pleasure in the pain, for who wants a lifetime of dreary lectures and homework from which the joy has been extracted? I would expect quality in an educational program whose students report that it is hard work, but meaningful and enjoyable too.

A high quality lifelong education also takes people "where they are." It recognizes that motivation to learn must accompany the act of formal

2. Alfred N. Whitehead, *The Aims of Education* (New York: Macmillan, 1929).

education; and its recognizes that, say, physics is not over if the twenty-year-old English major could not care less about it. After all, education has another fifty years, on the average, to raise that person's interest in physics. A program of high quality lifelong education teaches when students express readiness and stirs and meets their interest as it arises. For example, a university near me would be geared to meet my present interest in ancient civilizations with a learning program better (for I'm more demanding now) than the ones I could have taken at eighteen.

Finally, I see nothing wrong in the current rush to embrace adult students if the embrace results in "higher" learning. An institution that is turning toward adults should sponsor serious staff development with respect to adult learning in general as well as that institution's adult learners. Curriculum, teaching, and evaluation must be adjusted to be suitable for adults and solid evidence gathered on meaningful educational outcomes attained among adult learners. With positive evidence, I'd have some confidence that high quality is in that school. Such matters are stressed in the Higher Learning for Diverse Adults project undertaken by the Institute for Academic Improvement. Whether the initial motivation to serve adults is noble or base would be much less my concern.

Developmental Education

Cognitive psychologists are telling us what Dewey knew in advance of most formal research on intellectual functioning. We are not blank slates or empty gas tanks eagerly awaiting an educational fill-up. We are active solvers of the problems put before us (by ourselves, as well as by others). We learn by seeing and doing. We progress from simple, dualistic thinking about truth and values to more complex relativistic processes, in Perry's terms.[3] We progress from memorization to comprehension to application to analysis to synthesis and evaluation, in Bloom's taxonomy.[4] Even the four-year-old, new research suggests, is learning language, not by simply hearing it, but by trying to express herself and then getting response. The child is actively solving communication problems and, to do so, needs interaction.

The influence of this finding—that we are developing problem solvers rather than passive receptacles—has immense importance for education.

3. William Perry, *Forms of Intellectual and Ethical Development in the College Years* (New York: Holt-Rinehart, 1970).

4. Benjamin Bloom, *Taxonomy of Educational Objectives: The Cognitive Domain* (New York: McKay, 1956).

Lecturers and professors who do their students' thinking for them are not evil, for they have their place when a student is either highly dependent on authority or at a point in problem solving where some outside expertise is needed. More fundamental than dispensing knowledge is assistance offered students to advance in intellectual and ethical problem solving. One can see the tie here to lifelong learning. The high quality educator ascertains the current concerns and developmental level of a student, then aids that student in solving those immediate problems while strengthening intellectual and ethical ability to solve later problems. Some semblance of this approach is used in traditional education: the "problem" is to get a high grade in this course. Such an artifice can get a student busy, but it does not promise much for a longer, let alone lifelong, interest in learning the subject once it is "passed" (read, "past"). Incidentally, this device may help explain why high test scores predict future test scores but little else.

Education for Each

Suppose we find an educational program committed to lifelong learning. Suppose it even holds intellectual and ethical development at heart. If its staff still assumes a student-is-a-student-is-a-student, I would not expect quality there. An institution's students, no matter how limiting its admissions criteria, are bound to be individuals. They differ in several dimensions, each important to effective education.

One such dimension has already been stated—learning objectives. Faculty members often ask me, How can we motivate our students? There are tricks for making something interesting. If students can see personal benefits from learning physics, can discover it is quite compatible with what they already know or believe, can experience it firsthand and find it reasonably easy to grasp step by step, that subject has a chance. Skillful persuasion can increase awareness and appreciation. But if the student is consumed with interest in learning something else or still finds physics boring or irrelevant or scary, save it! Instead, discover what does interest the student and is within your definition of valuable education; then start there. Quality education theory has a chance, for it is pursued by a committed learner.

A second profound difference among students is that they do not all learn in the same way. Some learn more through concrete experience than through abstractions, whereas others thrive on conceptualization.[5] Some

5. David Kolb, *Learning Style Inventory* (Boston: McBer, 1976).

learn best in interactive groups whereas others like to learn alone.[6] Some are comfortable with people; some, with ideas; and some, with things.[7] A faculty that recognizes the learning styles of individual students and varies the curriculum and teaching to respond to those styles is a faculty likely to produce quality in education. A faculty that enables students to broaden their effective learning styles so that they are as comfortable with concepts as with "real life" action, as comfortable with other learners as alone—that faculty, in my opinion, is especially strong. Effective problem solving usually requires a wide repertoire of learning styles.

A third difference among students that is of vital importance has been noted: developmental level. The student who is highly dependent on authority and dualistic in thinking must be approached differently from the person who is autonomous and relativistic in thinking. The relativist who relies mainly on logic and general evidence will have to be approached somewhat differently from a person who relies heavily on context in order to determine what is true, beautiful, or right. Moreover, in order to bestir a student from fearful dependence on authority to principled autonomy (a frequently stated educational purpose), it helps to know where each person is on the developmental continuum. The educational program whose staff can describe the developmental level of each student and has skill in raising that developmental level is likely to be a program of high quality. A program that displays evidence of educational achievement for most students throughout a range of developmental stages and that also shows evidence of moving students to higher developmental stages, that program too is a quality educational program.

A fourth critical difference among students is background, socioeconomic as well as educational. At one time, most college students came from the white middle and upper classes. Now some are black, yellow, red, brown; some are dirt poor or first-generation middle income; some speak standard American and some speak very differently; some have family and community backgrounds in the subjects covered in schoolbooks, while others have little familiarity with the world their teachers know. Some were good in mathmatics but poor in English; others have thrived on social studies but dreaded chemistry. An educational program that treats all students or even categories of students (honors students, dis-

6. Anthony Grasha and Sheryl Riechmann, "Student Learning Styles Questionnaire," in *A Handbook for Faculty Development*, ed. William Bergquist and Stephen Phillips (Washington: Council for the Advancement of Small Colleges, 1975), pp. 32–44.

7. Patricia K. Cross, *Accent on Learning* (San Francisco: Jossey-Bass, 1976).

advantaged students) alike is a program from which I would expect high quality *for relatively few of its students*.

A fifth important difference among students might be termed "circumstances." Some students have job and family responsibilities while going to school; others do not. Some are in a stable period in their lives; others are amid the turmoil of transitions. Some must commute long distances; others live on campus. Some have friends and family who support their studies; others must go it alone, even in the face of ridicule. These are not small matters. A good educational program must attend to differing learner circumstances.

These five categories of important learner differences do not exhaust the list, but do seem to me to make enough demands on institutions that have ignored most of them. If an institution knows, and intentionally responds to, individual student differences in learning objectives, styles, developmental levels, backgrounds, and circumstances. I would expect it to be of high quality.

Collaborative Education

One way to misread my formula for high quality education in the 1980s is that it is permissive. If a student doesn't want to learn some hard and important preparatory subject now, don't press. There's a lifetime ahead. If the student functions at a low level of intellectual and ethical development, that's fine; accommodate to that level. If the objectives are too narrow or diffuse, the learning style too limited to allow the student to be an effective problem solver in various situations, if the background is weak and the circumstances difficult, who cares? Let that student decide how, what, and how much will be learned. To fight such predilections is fruitless.

That perspective is not mine, but is how progressive education got to be permissive education.[8] I would not expect much quality in a permissive school. Nor would I expect quality in an authoritarian institution that either disregarded individual differences or applied some pat formula. The word I see emerging most consistently from educational theory and practice is "collaboration." Learning emerges from a partnership, a hardheaded but humane negotiation between educator and student. In that relationship, I would expect to see the educator move toward individual learner objectives, styles, levels of development, circumstances; but I also would expect students to move toward the educator's more experienced, more developed

8. John Dewey, *Experience and Education* (New York: Macmillan, 1938).

sense of what needs to be learned, how, how much, and at what level. Thus is a student met where he is on his path of lifelong development but nudged, cajoled, and guided farther along not only in career but also in the intellectual and ethical contributions which can raise not only that person's life but other lives as well. It is in this encouragement to rise above a lower path, and the skill to aid the climb, that the quality of education finally resides.

Implementing Lifelong Development for Each

Traditional educators may find my definition of quality improbable. After all, who can promise lifelong development for each? Admittedly, it is a higher calling for educators as well as for students. Fortunately, we have our own mentors with whom to collaborate. Research and theory are appearing in support of lifelong, developmental, and individualized education, and many promising innovations are under way. Some traditional institutions, such as Michigan State University, are committed by policy to lifelong education in every department and college. Others, such as Goddard College, are committed to developmental education. And still others, such as Empire State College, have as their mission individualization at costs comparable to traditional approaches.

Enough is known about lifelong education for each that we can go forward with it. And we know far more than ever before about how to initiate change. If we and our colleagues steep ourselves in what is now known about lifelong education for each and how to bring it off, genuine quality in education can happen.

Collaborative Problem Solving

Theory and practice in planning and implementing change has proceeded in the same direction as educational theory and practice. The message is, treat your colleagues as you would your students, as active problem solvers who need the same nurture and challenge as the students. The task for the educational leader is, in a word, to collaborate.[9]

The term "collaboration" evokes assumptions of naïveté that we can reach consensus and that, if left alone, faculty or students will attain high quality education by themselves. Forget that view of collaboration. Instead, picture strong *leadership* with strong *involvement*. They are requisites to quality.

9. Jack Lindquist, *Strategies for Change* (Washington: Council for the Advancement of Small Colleges, 1978).

How can we create this new kind of collaboration? Again, recent theory and practice come to our aid. As I synthesized in *Strategies for Change*, five ingredients mark the organization that is well equipped to develop and renew quality—continuously: a skillful and active *force* for improvement; strong *linkage* of organization members to one another, to the knowledge bases needed for recognizing the need for change and for producing promising solutions, and to the whole problem-solving process; genuine *openness* in reaching out to discover problems and find solutions; equally strong *ownership* of change by those who must carry it out as well as back it; and *rewards* commensurate with the effort and skill put into development or renewal.

A quick look at most institutions reveals that few people devote much time or skill to improvement. Implementing the *status quo* and fighting brushfires preoccupy them. Faculty members, administrators, and other staff are weakly linked to one another, to useful information, or to decision making. Closed minds to new ideas or opposing views are more common than open ones. By the time most so-called improvements reach implementation, they have been so compromised that nobody feels much commitment to or ownership of them. And rewards? Advocates for improvement work overtime, neglect more extrinsically rewarding activities such as publication, experience frustration if not attack, and too often are turned down for promotion while those who play the traditional games get ahead.

We are discovering ways to strengthen all five factors that help promote quality education. Staff in most institutions includes administrators whose job descriptions incorporate some responsibility for program and staff development. In general, teachers are expected to engage in some committee work and their own professional development. Offices for improvement aids such as institutional research, academic planning, and professional development are fairly common. Often, an elaborate governance system exists, and usually at least some funds are available for program and professional development.

In short, a potential force for improvement exists, but the people involved are likely to be untrained, uncoordinated, unsupported, and undermined, with the members operating on outmoded notions about change. A first leadership task is to identify this potential force and then give it systematic training in collaborative problem solving, in combining strong leadership with strong involvement. One of the best devices for training is to have members collaborate in the context of real program and professional problem solving, rather than in unarticulated training programs. And as in education, the development of a force is not simply preparatory and terminal, but rather continuous as new people are added, new skills are developed, and new challenges are confronted.

One leadership task is to strengthen the continuing learning of organization members, together, *about education*. The job is to create an educational network as strong as disciplinary networks (without challenging the latter, which also are crucial). Who are our students? How are they doing? What new challenges face education here and elsewhere? What innovations are rising to meet those challenges, with what success? Linkage devices include local data gathering and sharing, workshops, group trips to educational conferences, availability of books and journals about education, sabbaticals, and formal or informal networks of persons concerned to learn together about how to improve educational quality. If budget cuts start with such "frills," the chance at quality is also cut. Perhaps the most effective tactic for strengthening linkage is to build that "force" slowly. In one university, for example, only ten faculty members a year receive support to learn together about their university, its students, its effectiveness, its context, and new alternatives in education; but after five years, this force is one-sixth of the faculty. It remains together through its Fellows Association; because its members hold many key university posts in governance and administration, the effect of their numbers is multiplied.

Linking staff to members of other departments or schools is one step toward greater openness. This ingredient is especially a frame of mind which leaders can create by their own open-mindedness. The leader who leans forward to listen, who circulates on campus rather than sitting in an office, who sincerely seeks to appreciate proposals contrary to his or her own conclusions, who encourages others to listen attentively to students and does so as well, who uses committee chairmanships to ensure that everyone has a say and is heard, who attends conferences and also sends others—that is a leader on the way to quality in education. Again, openness does not mean nonassertion of one's own thinking. The nondirective leader is likely to get the institution moving in no direction. One critical skill is to communicate in ways that increase openness to the leader's own ideas. Two-way openness becomes a cornerstone to quality, whether in a teacher-student or a president-faculty relationship. It is worth taking time to learn how much openness is present (especially in the opinion of others) and to learn how to increase one's own and others' openness.

Why do we imagine that our version of quality can be forced on students or faculty who hold quite different views? We know we cannot *make* faculty members teach, in new ways, well; we simply do not have the control, and teaching well requires the commitment of the teacher. Also (no small also), teachers, like students, have much knowledge to contribute to our definition of quality education.

The leader task, then, is to *share* but not give up the ownership of improvement. The point is to increase the number of members who feel that local improvements are, at least partially, their solutions (or ones they accept) to problems they perceive in pursuit of goals they value. Effective linking activities openly practiced by the institution's growing force for improvement contribute to broadening the sense of ownership. Professional development practices that incorporate both the professional's own improvement agenda and the agenda of the institution also promote joint negotiated ownership. Academic goal setting and curricular planning initiated by administrators, led by a planning committee and involving faculty members as well as students each step of the way, also reflect ownership. Examples in *Strategies for Change* include Messiah College and the University of South Carolina; other promising models can be found at the University of Akron, Wichita State University, Furman University, and Austin College.

Rewards

Educational leaders point out that if improving educational quality goes unrewarded, improvement goes nowhere. Only lately, however, have leaders overhauled reward systems in order to buttress quality and instituted new means to assess and reward effective teaching. New ways to assess program effectiveness now permit more general payoffs for those laboring in that program. Educators are discovering the value of social rewards—personal thanks and acknowledgment of accomplishment can make the drudgery of change worth while. Support groups become sources of reward for persons courageous enough to buck a complacent status quo. New ways to lead committees and to assign workload are making involvement in educational improvement less burdensome and more enjoyable than it was. As consumerism and funder accountability grow, demonstrated quality in lifelong development for each may well increase institutional funding, rewards until now reserved mainly for demonstrated quality in research and scholarship, not in teaching.

In short, the set of ingredients here suggested for effective initiation and implementation of quality improvements in education is not only supported by change research but also demonstrated in practice. A strong and open improvement force, whose members are well linked in their relationship and in information, owned both by leaders and others, and rewarding to those involved, can be developed. Indeed, in my view, such a force must be created if continuing advances in lifelong development for each are to occur.

Black Colleges—
Living with the New Realities

ISAAC H. MILLER, JR.

THE MISSION STATEMENTS of any group of small colleges will, in general, reveal a consensus of what should be the outcomes of quality education, and each college can lay claim to some degree of success in achieving the established goals with a given client population. Traditionally, college administrators have been rather smug in assessing the quality of their institutions, and the statements have been accepted without much challenge. If, however, current trends continue, the students of the future will increasingly demand value received for value offered—truth in advertising—with an assertiveness unaccustomed in the higher education community. Today, all colleges function in an unusual environment in which a set of complex new variables is imposing new priorities and imperatives.

Though colleges and universities annually confer degrees on scores of graduates, evan a casual analysis would indicate that a substantial proportion of the graduates are ill-equipped to compete with peers in the marketplace. The outcomes of the experience are frequently short of the mark because the students' needs and limitations had never been carefully assessed. In the present societal setting, the traditional approaches to teaching may prove ineffective or only marginally successful. College professors confronting the enormity of the new needs may experience sagging enthusiasm. On the other hand, the true educator will realize that developing new instructional strategies to achieve quality education represents the newest and most exciting frontier in postsecondary education.

The environment in which the youth of America are educated is frequently inhospitable to serious scholarly endeavor. It is an environment of many contradictions: Excellence is extolled as a virtue, but the rewards of being average are frequently greater. There is the promise of opportunity for all, but the reality is that the door may open to only a gifted few. For many, it is an environment of confused implications, partially fulfilled pledges, frustrations, and many distractions.

The problems that face youth generally are especially acute for black youth who seek access to the mainstream of the American enterprise. Although many enter college well prepared and highly motivated, others bear the permanent scars and negative effects from a desegregation process in the public school system that in many instances went awry. Many black youth are inadequately equipped to advance because they are deficient in communication and computation skills. Many enter college with negative self-concepts and limited desire to excel. Many have reached college lacking the positive influence of successful heads-of-families as role models. Many feel that no matter how well educated they may become, the system is really not for them. For all of these, the black college becomes a type of extended family where in loco parentis has a special meaning.

Black colleges, conceived in the black experience, address the foregoing concerns more directly than do other institutions of the higher education community. They accept a disproportionate share of the responsibility for encouraging and motivating promising young blacks who may be under-prepared emotionally and academically to negotiate the higher education ladder. The insights, creativity, and resourcefulness historically found in the faculties of black colleges are increasingly needed throughout American higher education today.

Quality education for the mass of black people will be provided as institutions accept their obligation to plow new ground, to discover and devise new measures for enhancing the prognosis of success for the individual student. Faculties will need to acknowledge that many of the accustomed academic constructs are inadequate to meet current and future needs. If the college is to fulfill its mission, teachers must reestablish themselves as mentors and the institution as a caring community.

Accepting the black college as having a unique mission in the higher education community, quality education is measured by the progress the student has made from entry to graduation, by performance on standardized graduate and professional school admissions tests, and by the confidence with which he moves and functions in the work force.

Living with the New Realities

For the foreseeable future, black colleges will be the point of entry into mainstream America for a substantial proportion of blacks. It is important to note that although only 30 percent of all blacks in postsecondary education attend historically black colleges; more than 50 percent of today's black graduates are produced by them. About seven out of ten blacks who enroll in white colleges never graduate. Nevertheless, the historically black college will experience increasing competition for the pool of black students.

Desegregation in the elementary and secondary school systems has had significant negative consequences that frequently leave the black student unready for traditional college work. In the future, as in the past, the black college will have to invest sizable resources in a broad range of supportive services just to get these students ready.

As state systems become increasingly concerned with economics and, in consequence, public policy in education is governed by these concerns, public black colleges will come under growing pressure to lose their ethnic identities.

Black colleges will experience heightened competition for foundation, corporate, other philanthropic, and federal support. Today, only 3 percent of the federal higher education dollar goes to this group of institutions.

During the 1960s, black colleges experienced a siphoning-off of experienced black teachers to white institutions which sought to comply with affirmative action guidelines and to satisfy the clamor of black students for a black professional presence. This trend will undergo some reversal, but it will take time before the black institutions regain their prior strength in master teachers, although strength in doctorates may improve.

As the competition for students increases, many talented blacks who would have chosen a black school will enroll in historically white institutions. One consequence will be the need for black colleges to increase their developmental programs, thus making quality education more time consuming and costly.

The New Imperatives

Black colleges, in common with other black institutions, will quite likely continue to live with the legacy of presumed inferiority; a legacy that creates difficulties for image building and resource procurement. The people who work in these institutions, despite being fully conscious of the foregoing, understand that quality education in all its dimensions remains the key to access for the black student. Acceptance of this verity is difficult for those who contend that the black institutions should be phased out, eliminated immediately, or converted to remedial institutions. Yet the distressing statistics on the number of blacks receiving bachelor's degrees from white colleges offer proof that the historically white institutions are not philosophically and practically prepared to supply the support measures needed to provide quality education for any appreciable increased number of black students from disadvantaged backgrounds.

In acknowledging their mission, it is incumbent on the black college to develop strategies for enhancing the learning skills of students and in the process to accelerate the learning process.

- Teachers must be encouraged and given incentive to become master teachers and prime movers. They must adopt measures that strengthen the student's self-concept and that develop a reverence for learning.
- The college must make a clear, unequivocal commitment to develop strong supportive strategies to correct the student's academic deficiencies.
- The college must free itself of nonproductive activities and situations so that its modest resources may be fully invested in providing the core services that clearly produce a competent, well adjusted student.
- The college will need to provide the support and the opportunity for teachers to take sabbatical and other short-term leave in order to pursue advanced degrees and other measures of professional renewal.
- The college must maintain such academic options as honors courses and scholars programs, as resources permit, in order to challenge the self-propelled student and to provide stimulation for the professor.
- A college with limited resources cannot assay to be all things to all comers. Hence, it is incumbent on the black college to select the major disciplines in which it will seek to stand out and, having done so, initiate a systematic program for faculty development in these areas.

The various innovations being employed in many black institutions to meet the new realities lie beyond the scope of the present discussion. However, as noted above, many black colleges measure institutional excellence according to what happens to the student. The crucial element in student success is effort, and attitude is crucial to effort. Introducing the student into a caring, disciplined environment is the first order of business in developing positive attitudes. Students with academic deficiencies will take on remedying their shortcomings when inspired and encouraged to do so by caring teachers. Colleges are discovering that positive peer influence for excellence and early academic success offer positive motivation. Although entry standards and advancement options may vary, the maintenance of high exit criteria and the performance of the graduate determine whether the student has had an educational experience of incontrovertible quality. The administration has heavy responsibility for providing and maintaining a creative forum through which all constituencies of the college embrace the new dimensions of responsibility with commitment.

It is implicit in these observations that effective performance in an area of national need should be improved and built upon. Black colleges represent a mechanism that can be strengthened and used to intensify the nation's effort to equalize opportunity.

2. QUALITY OF ADMINISTRATION— ARE LEADERSHIP AND NO GROWTH COMPATIBLE?

Leadership for Academic Growth

DONALD E. WALKER

ARE LEADERSHIP AND NO GROWTH COMPATIBLE? For colleges and universities, the question is as difficult to answer as it is important to ask. At
one extreme, the bracing rhetoric of obligatory optimism says, Of course
leadership is possible in any situation; all we need is great leaders. At the
other extreme is monumental gloom, with its cliché of pessimism, I am
tired of dealing with ruthless hope; we're in trouble— bad trouble—and
we may as well admit it. In the final analysis, we shall probably simply
have to live our way through to the answers, and they will be plural rather
than singular.

Two Types of Leadership

I shall bypass defining "leadership," "quality," and "quality administration" and, instead, make some assumptions and offer some propositions.
I suspect that leadership in the no-growth situation in which we in colleges
and universities will find ourselves in the coming years will be characterized
by two thrusts.

At one pole, "strong leaders" will develop who will administer with
relatively authoritarian styles. They will use the higher level of consent
to authority present in the society in crisis situations to impose "order"
and a kind of coherence on academic communities. This kind of leadership
will be popular with a segment of the public and indeed with a few of the
constituencies on campus. It will at least supress some of the more gaudy
manifestations of academic infighting and give the appearance of positive
movement. For example, when budgets are discussed, there will be crisp
decision points to talk about. The public will be assured that someone is
"in charge." I further assume that a price will be paid for such leadership
styles. Faculties will drift toward adversary employee-employer relationships with their institutions. Many of the more creative, cutting-edge
minds, rather than become enmeshed in this tangle, may simply go
elsewhere. There are subtle qualities about a university that are nonne-

29

gotiable. If conditions are favorable, they exist. If unfavorable, they will not.

At the other pole will be the more democratic-political styles of leadership. This style recognizes the real division of power within the university and draws fully on the multitude of talents present in any academic community. Fundamental to this style are open communications and the building of trust. The major process is that of team problem solving. A major goal is to build consensus. Here too, there will be a price to pay. Movement under such a style appears slow and cumbersome. Decisions are not crisp, although they tend to have more staying power. Strident and dissenting voices on campuses will be more audible, and many outside constituencies of the university will protest the seeming noise and confusion. Despite the drawbacks, I propose that democratic-political styles of leadership offer the most realistic hope for quality administration in tight fiscal circumstances.

Under either authoritarian or democratic leadership in times of financial crisis, I predict that presidents will turn over more frequently. After all, there are no heroes in tough times.

From Leader to Leadership

One of the toughest situations leaders will have to avoid is the lifeboat psychology that sacrifices everything to survival. It is too easy, under these circumstances, to sacrifice quality in an effort to stay afloat. Obviously some quality must go. But the leaders will have to be more enterprising and come up with more imaginative solutions to our problems. Where do such imaginative ideas come from? The conventional view says they come from brilliant, imaginative leaders. I think not. Rather, I believe, they come from leaders who know how to tap the brilliance and imagination that surrounds them. At any rate, in seeking imaginative solutions to the problems of low budget, I propose that we have to draw on those who are closer to the problem. Learning to tap the talent of the faculty and others on campus calls for a democratic-political style of leadership. Several propositions may help in an understanding of the complexities of the situation.

1. The general attitudes toward leadership that prevail in the society are frequently reflected on the campuses. The trend in the United States today is for people to feel closer to equality with their leaders. The awe is gone; the era of the charismatic leader is waning. They are less willing today than in the past to surrender their fate uncritically to a leader.

(Higher education may have had something to do with this change in attitude, but that is another story.)

In the case of leadership today, what is true of society applies even more strongly to the university, where the dealings are with equals who most definitely see themselves that way. Dealing with equals within higher education institutions presents more difficulties than when the leadership dealings are with the broader society where a proportion of the populace view themselves as being in the hands of experts and specialists who are at least wiser, in a specific field, than they. In the latter cases, the crisis of leadership that thus evolves is one of trust—if not a conviction that decisions are always right—that the decisions are being made for the correct reasons and in the proper spirit of concern for all. Such trust has to be won, not once, but constantly.

2. The problem for leadership in colleges and universities then may well be the creation of consensus, rather than the administration of con sensus. The crisis is less one of leadership than of followership.

3. It has been said that this nation is a society between clarifying ideals. In part, the crisis in values arises as a condition of a search for a sense of direction. This condition also holds true in the university. The liberal arts—in my view, the heart of the university—are noticeable between clarifying ideals. The pressures on the university in a no-growth situation may not be evenly distributed. The humanities and the liberal arts generally may well receive an exorbitant share of the pressure.

4. According to common observation, leadership at the present time tends to coalesce around movements rather than persons—the environmental movement, the women's movement, even the physical fitness movement. Leadership itself has become relatively anonymous. John Kenneth Galbraith has said, "Fifty years ago, everyone knew who was the head of Ford, IBM, or General Motors. Now, nobody knows. What you get is collectivity."[1] As applied to the campus in a no-growth situation, the most effective leadership will, I suspect, emphasize the process of decision making and involvement of people in the solutions rather than press specific answers that come down from the top. The cult of personality simply will not avail among cynical and sorely pressed academics.

5. One of our problems may be that we have grown accustomed to considering "growth" and "expansion" as synonymous. They are not. Growth can take place without adding to something. This is both "good

1. Lance Morrow, "A Cry for Leadership," *Time*, August 6, 1979, p. 28.

news and bad news," however. The good news is that the institution doesn't have to stand still simply because something cannot be added. The bad news is that the process is far more difficult than the kind of growth institutions and their faculties have become accustomed to. It is far easier, for example, to add a major in environmental management than it is to subtract a major in, say, Latin American studies and replace it with one in environmental management. But because such changes will be so difficult to deal with, the building of trust will be essential. These kinds of decisions demand a democratic, consultative style of leadership; otherwise, the result will be low morale, frustration, and, eventually, disruptions.

Specifically, trust and the credibility of leadership will turn in large part on the ways in which a number of critical decisions are handled. Some significant examples are the fixing of priorities for cutbacks and budget reductions when they must occur; the extent to which these decisions are shared with faculty, staff, and sometimes students; the way decisions on tenure and promotion are handled; and finally, the way in which grievances are managed.

Effective leadership styles must call forth higher levels of consent in these areas. The quality of a university in the final analysis is the result of an act of will by the members of that community. Just as money alone cannot summon excellence, the absence of resources alone cannot kill the spirit of a university unless the members of that academic community are accomplices to that act.

The love of learning has flourished in poverty and deprivation. It has survived even the dark night of barbarism. The will to achieve and the refusal to be deflected or put off is inner-directed. Effective administration will draw its true strength from these internal resources and, where successful, will see that the credit is given to those who truly deserve it. This course may not seem like the heroic model of leadership our society has come to expect, but I believe it is model that will work best.

Presidential Leadership for the 1980s

JOSEPH F. KAUFFMAN

THE CONVENTIONAL ASSUMPTIONS about higher education in the next decade include (1) a decline in the number of students attending college;

(2) increasing economic problems owed in part to energy costs and inflation; and (3) a lowered sense of the value of, or priority of support for, higher education. The changing demographic facts will, however, not affect all institutions uniformly. In some areas of the country, the number of eighteen-year-olds will increase in the 1980s. In some sun-belt states, new campuses will have to be built. Within states, some institutions will lose students while others will grow. Some of the effects will depend on institutional responsiveness to the needs of nontraditional students and new groups of traditional-age students.

As for inflation and energy problems, both residential institutions far from metropolitan areas and large urban institutions accessible by mass transportation will experience the changing conditions but in quite different ways. The assumption about a lowered sense of value in, or support for, higher education will, I contend, be greatly affected by the quality and vigor of leadership in our institutions and systems. In short, the environment will be far more turbulent than steady state.

There is not much joy in being a college president today. A principal frustration is all the external constraints placed on presidents. In many ways and areas, presidential judgment and discretion have been greatly reduced or eliminated through the adoption of uniform procedures, formulas, and policies which command our fealty more than our good sense. As Ashworth observed, "Like Pavlov's dogs, administrators bit by bit are being conditioned to stay within very limited and well-trodden paths by shocks, commands, intimidations, and orders."[1]

To the other constraints must be added the decade or more of anti-establishment fervor with its concomitant hostility toward our social institutions and their leaders. I have no doubt, however, that the pendulum is swinging to a more positive view about the need for leadership and the renewal of our social institutions. Americans can be pessimistic for only so long; then they want to get going and do something affirmative. This change is why I believe sensitive and optimistic leadership is so necessary for the 1980s.

Relationship with Faculty

The major concern I have about the internal environment of higher education in the decade ahead relates to faculties—the teacher-scholars.

1. Kenneth H. Ashworth, *American Higher Education in Decline* (College Station: Texas A&M Press, 1979), p. 89.

There are two matters I wish to identify: faculty self-esteem and morale, and the danger of treating the faculty as scapegoat.

In the past decade colleges and universities experienced an attack on both the liberal arts and the Western, rationalistic, scientific, and technological approach to knowledge and experience. The bench mark of relevance was also invoked. Faculty worth was measured by the immediate utility to which their knowledge could be put. In the late 1960s, the frame of reference was peace, the solution of urban problems, racism, and poverty. Currently, there is a wave of enrollment shifts to professional and applied subjects. Concern is less with a subject's relevance to a social revolution than it is an assessment of a subject's utility in the job market. In my opinion, this trend too will change.

The point in this portrayal is that our faculties have, in many ways, suffered a lengthy period of demoralization that affects their sense of commitment, pride in their work, and satisfaction with their career choice and its pursuit. Many faculty members were once applauded for possessing competence in areas or subjects now seen as arcane. It is difficult for a faculty member to celebrate having committed his or her life to being a scholar-teacher, only to find that, rather than the intrinsic value of that devotion being sufficient, professional worth is also being assessed by the declining number of student credit hours produced. Being good at something no one seems to value provides little satisfaction.

The lack of faculty mobility, the so-called Ph.D. glut, adds to the problem. Perceptive presidents have described to me, in poignant terms, the bitterness and hostility they perceive in some faculty members who feel trapped in teaching in an institution they never regarded as more than a stepping-stone. Such persons, seeing no alternative to remaining for the rest of their professional careers in institutions they view as out of phase with their aspirations and talents, lash out at both administrators and students. Alienated from both their institutions and authority, they become the leaders of faculty councils and unions. Yet they are the principal group to whom a new president must turn in seeking to renew an institution.

The second part of this problem I identified as the danger of treating the faculty as scapegoat. The result may be to reinforce the negative aspects of faculty morale, described above. Here, I refer to the faculty, particularly tenured faculty members, being regarded as a *problem*, because they are not easily dismissed or interchanged with new or younger or different faculty. It is not unusual to hear tenure attacked or senior faculty portrayed as deadwood. The howls of some institution leaders when retirement age was extended to seventy was indicative of the message, We wish we didn't have to keep you so long, and if you would leave, we could bring in more vital people (at less salary) to invigorate us. Often administrators and board members respond to criticism of their institution's inertia by blaming the faculty as a group of reactionaries who, protected by tenure, resist any innovation or modernization. Obviously, there are persons who fit such a description. Yet, on the whole, we add to the problem by oversimplifying it and resorting to stereotyping faculty as recalcitrant foes of renewal and improvement. What is needed is a kind of leadership that intervenes in this vicious circle and begins to lift us out of our predicament. The leader who is primarily motivated to avoid personal blame is not needed. Too many others are using that script.

There are many good reasons for the faculties to feel as they do about their institutions and their leaders. If they are made culprit in our time of trouble, to whom can we turn for improving our condition? The faculty is the core of the higher education enterprise. Without them, there is no enterprise.

The Leadership Needed

In my view, colleges and universities need politically effective leadership, visible leadership, and leadership that cherishes the essential value of our educational institutions and their potential for dignifying life and shaping the larger destiny. Only with such leadership can we release the creative energies within our institutions that are the solution to our problem.

The word "political" is often used pejoratively. That connotation is unfortunate here because politically effective leadership is necessary, particularly in the vast public sector of higher education. A president should know what is needed in the way of public support and be effective in the extent to which he or she can build support for those needs.

The low-profile president may have been of value during the past decade. I believe we need visible leadership now—leaders who will teach the public—what James MacGregor Burns terms "transforming" leadership. Although Burns was writing about political rather than educational leaders, his view is germane to the point I make.

> Leaders can also shape and alter and elevate the motives and values and goals of followers through the vital *teaching* role of leadership. This is *transforming* leadership. The premise of this leadership is that, whatever the separate interests persons might hold, they are presently or potentially united in the pursuit of

"higher" goals, the realization of which is tested by the achievement of significant change that represents the collective or pooled interests of leaders and followers.[2]

There is, of course, risk in being a visible leader and attempting to be a transforming leader. But in the years ahead we in higher education will be sorely tested. If we believe that our institutions have value, we must articulate that value and achieve adequate understanding and support. We must find leaders who are dedicated enough to the purpose of higher education that they will expend themselves, if necessary, for that purpose.

A period of lower student enrollments will, in my opinion, not harm us. Nor do I believe that financial austerity will destroy us. In many ways, it would be healthy for us to be required to revisit and redefine the essence of our enterprise. We have gone through three decades of expansion, accommodating growth. We could use a breathing period to examine our deficits in quality and sort out our priorities. If necessary, we could get back to the basic purposes of the university, from which we are often distracted.

The skills of management are not to be demeaned for they are crucial to implementing great purposes. But by themselves they will be insufficient for the turbulent period ahead. In the conflict over the allocation of public resources to the various social needs of society, and in the conflict over reduction and reallocation within our colleges and universities there will be considerable anguish. Political skill will be desirable. The indispensable ingredient of leadership will be a sense of trust that the leader will do the *right* thing with what limited discretion remains. Leadership of this kind understands and is committed to the values that people of the best motives can follow. It means an appreciation of the essence of our colleges and universities and why they were created and supported and esteemed for so many generations. It means leadership which will not confuse service and training and practical relevance of some courses (important as that might be) with the even more important concern for the cultivation of serious knowledge, a concern with beauty, truth, justice, and life itself.

I am speaking of leaders who understand and care deeply about what Edward Shils calls the "capital" of a university:

> That capital is much more than its physical plant or its library; it is also more than the stock of knowledge and skills that its academic staff members bring to their tasks. It includes the zeal for discovery, the normal integrity, the powers of discriminating judgment, the awareness of important problems, and the

2. *Leadership* (New York: Harper & Row, 1978), pp. 425–26.

possibilities for their solution that their members possess. These are qualities of individuals, but their stable persistence depends on the existence of an academic community, within departments and faculties in the university as a whole and in the academic community at large—within the boundaries of the country and internationally.[3]

The president will have to take initiatives, the consequences of which are important. Mistakes are easily covered in times of growth. That escape will be less easy in the future. When I speak of "visible and transforming leadership," I am not making that a feat of derring do or even confusing it with personal charisma. I mean those qualities that restore in organizations or society a sense of meaning and purpose and that release the powerful capacity humankind has for renewal.

I believe higher education and colleges and universities to be important to our future. There is some legitimacy to demands that we be consumer-oriented, productivity-conscious, and output-oriented. Yet we know the matter is more complex and more important than those demands imply.

While I do not equate the importance of presidents with the importance of the higher education enterprise, nevertheless I do believe that the kind of leadership I have described is crucial to the future of our institutions. There are no material incentives to attract the kind of dedicated service I believe necessary. Rather, a sense of service is required—a sense of service that links leaders with fundamental and serious matters that have concerned good men and women for centuries in the past and will continue to do so in the future.

Hard Times—
Catalyst for Leadership Development

PAUL C. GIANINI, JR.

THE IMMENSE GROWTH of community colleges in numbers and in enrollments during the 1950s and 1960s stemmed from the view that almost everyone needed to attend college either to pursue a baccalaureate degree or to be trained to qualify as a technician in one of myriad areas. Enrollments in public two-year colleges in 1967 reached 1.5 million and by 1977 had risen to more than 4 million. In 1977–79, according to estimates, enrollments of persons age thirty-five and over grew by at least one-third, with

3. "Governments and Universities," in *The University and the State: What Role for Government in Higher Education?* ed. Sidney Hook, Paul Kurtz, and Miro Todorovich (Buffalo: Prometheus Books, 1978), pp. 20–21.

the rate of increase greater for women than for men.[1] For more than two decades, colleges and universities had as major problems the overcrowding of residence halls, the building of new facilities, creation of new programs, and other matters characteristic of a growth period and summarized as problems "we like to have."

In the 1970s, enrollment trends changed, and the problems suddenly were serious, even threatening the survival of some institutions that had until recently enjoyed success. The quest began for services to students from "new populations." Legislative bodies dealing with postsecondary education finances started inquiring into the results being achieved by institutions. Legislatures in some states felt compelled to become involved in day-to-day operation of colleges and passed laws that prohibited closed meetings of boards and that permitted legislative participation in decision making at the local level. Retrenchment impinged on faculty members, whose worries about salary demands and working conditions led to growth in faculty unionism. In turn, unionism has impinged on many areas of administrative authority and decision.

As the problems mounted in the 1970s, management of decline and formal planning processes became principal topics. Many optimistic administrators saw the steady state or shrinkage as a move toward excellence and tried to persuade their constituencies about the values of long-range planning. But the reversal in enrollments had caught institutions off guard, and the planning efforts were too little and too late. According to Naor, long-range planning is at a crossroads.[2] Its value and effectiveness are being questioned by many, particularly the crises in energy and material shortages came to most planners as a surprise if not shock. Planning in an environment of increasing uncertainty often is said to make the process a costly exercise in futility.[3] While Naor's frame of reference is the business world, the same problems apply in education. We are constantly being surprised, and our poor record in gaining favorable legislation and increased funding, together with the lack of leadership, are principal shortcomings.

Planning

As Richardson sees the situation, some administrators now assume that the need for planning has lessened inasmuch as the undertakings planned

1. *Community, Junior and Technical College Directory, 1978* (Washington: American Association of Community and Junior Colleges).

2. Jacob Naor, "Planning by Consensus: A Participative Approach to Planning," *S.A.M. Advanced Management Journal;* American Management Associations, Autumn 1978.

3. Ibid., p. 40.

stand little likelihood of obtaining funding.[4] He is probably right. Under current planning procedures, usually the general objectives and planning guidelines are formulated by first- and second-echelon administrators and receive approval from the board of trustees. These are then transmitted to the rest of the organization, which, in turn, prepare three- to five-year plans with some degree of specificity. The plans then go back to the management for review and approval. Normally, reviews are held annually and plans are revised at least annually. This stereotyped planning process has its drawbacks. The relationship between the board, the president and his staff, and the rest of the institution is sporadic and communications are lacking. This type of planning leads to the most attention being given to immediate crises. There is no set procedure that encourages contributions to the planning. Finally, beyond the president and his staff, there is no real commitment to the plan.

Community colleges have always regarded planning as a means toward orderly expansion. Now it is viewed as a means to anticipate rather than react to crises, which seem to occur with increasing frequency and severity. Both programs and increase in the number of institutions have been curtailed. Planning has been done on both the local and state levels, with states attempting to equalize access to programs in higher education throughout their state. For example, the Ohio Board of Regents in 1975 published the findings on its two-year college system in a planning report that emphasized areas where unwarranted program duplication and unnecessary institutional competition existed.[5] Further, professionals are beginning to differ with the belief that the community college will continue to grow indefinitely. While a moratorium on new community colleges is often unpopular, fiscal realities may warrant it for several reasons: the number of potential community college students in decreasing; the value of a college education is being more severely questioned; and the unserved populations become fewer in number. At the same time, business and industry are entering the education market, the archetypal example being the American Telephone and Telegraph Company, which has a larger education budget than any college or university in our country and does not heavily stress degrees as valuable to advancement in its organization.

Two major problems hamper the planning process. The first is the lack

4. Richard C. Richardson, "Adapting to Declining Resources Through Planning and Research," in *Coping with Reduced Resources*, ed. Richard L. Alfred (San Francisco: Jossey-Bass, 1978).

5. *The Two-Year College System in Ohio: A Planning Report* (Columbus: Ohio Board of Regents, 1975).

of reliable data on which to make decisions; the second is the absence of systematic analyses to translate raw data into usable information. A third factor—sometimes the most devastating—is political reverberations. For example, the five-year plan for California community colleges for 1976–81 clearly indicated a philosophical base emphasizing their role as community-based institutions of lifelong learning. The 1976 master plan for these colleges showed that 440 new academic and vocational programs were scheduled for the following year. In the middle of this plan, Proposition 13 was passed. Soon afterward, the California legislature curtailed further expansion of adult education. Fortunately, institutional pressure and continued public support prevented substantial reduction; yet it is doubtful that the 440 new programs were initiated. Although the California legislature staved off the full effects of Proposition 13 through distribution of a budget surplus, the true effects will soon be felt.[6]

Adult education receives wide public support and is growing faster than any other level of education. But legislators have not been persuaded to fund activities in this area. Thus, adult education is still perceived as being marginal in nature, carried on through evening colleges and a series of extension activities, as opposed to the major thrust of the community college segment.

The political realities of our times must be considered if we are to succeed in our attempts to secure favorable action for community colleges through both procedures of state departments and laws proposed by our legislators. In 1924, Koos wrote that the policy of generous encouragement from the state implied a state system of junior college units, which should be carried through as economically and efficiently to the state and its youth as possible.[7] Although few would disagree with Koos's statement, there is less and less agreement about state financing of community colleges and the strings tied to it. The drift toward state and federal dominance and away from local control has increased dramatically, and in some states, such as Florida, complaints are heard that the state legislators are participating in the day-to-day operation of institutions of higher education.

College leaders must be prepared to affirm the purpose and scope of their institutions to state and federal legislators. Governing boards are assuming administrative functions; collective bargaining is diminishing the

6. Ami Zusman, "State Policy Making for Community College Adult Education," *Journal of Higher Education*, July-August 1978, pp. 337–57.

7. Leonard V. Koos, "The Junior College," vol. 2, Research Publications of the University of Minnesota (Minneapolis: University of Minnesota, 1924).

power of centralized administration; and diminishing enrollments and the decline in dollars, combined with rising costs, create a quandary. Political realities must be considered. Thus far, there is little conflict among elementary, secondary, and higher education, but also little cooperation. We are as guilty as the policy makers because we seldom recognize this relationship as worthy of attention.

When the educators cannot answer our legislators' questions, we invite external intervention and domination. Colleges must be able to measure outcomes and present the results in an organized and factual manner so as to secure external support. It is most distressing when state boards know more about the outcomes of programs offered by the colleges than do the colleges themselves.

Some states have avoided such conflicts. In Oklahoma, the statewide plan for junior college education included demographic studies of current and future populations, socioeconomic patterns of enrollments, manpower distribution and needs, existing and required educational services (including elementary and secondary schools), financing, and, most important, the articulation of two-year colleges with other state institutions of higher education.[8] Would that such studies were undertaken in all the states.

Growth—No Growth

The workshops in marketing, development, recruitment, et cetera, advertised in the *Chronicle of Higher Education* evidence the vigorous competition for the declining number of potential students. I think we need to accept as fact that the days of colleges being "bigger and better" are over. No longer do we pride ourselves on large enrollment increases annually. No longer can we rely on the successes and phenomenal growth of our institutions to allow our management and our styles to go unquestioned. Mistakes are no longer tolerated, and the days of perfunctory administration have ended.

Rather, we find ourselves forced to make change by substitution as opposed to addition. The very question of the value of postsecondary education is at the forefront. Uncertainty about its economic benefits is but one factor in the declining image of the institution of higher education. Indeed, it appears that colleges are responding more to the marketplace

---

8. *Junior College Education in Oklahoma: A Report of a State-Wide Study* (Oklahoma City: Oklahoma State Regents for Higher Education, February 1970).

than to the true educational needs of our society or to the philosophy underlying our institutions.

We in education have tried to emulate business planning but with only partial success: our "goods" cannot be put into a production line and bear the guarantee of the producer. Many recent policy changes in American higher education have failed to enhance educational programs and in some cases have contributed to their deterioration. We have placed increasing reliance on financial aid. We have deemphasized the residential college. We have seen single-sex colleges merge and become coeducational, a move that only relocates the available pool of students. And we have allowed ourselves to be tried by the media—an always risky position.

Leadership is needed now more than at any other time in American educational history. We face a new set of problems for which the past gives insufficient guidance. We must explore more thoroughly other areas such as governmental domains, cooperation with external forces such as unions, and new partnerships with our colleagues in elementary and secondary education. Only through this style of collaboration will we in higher education be able to provide the sorely needed leadership.

Some Administrative Conditions for Survival

JOHN W. NASON

THE QUESTION "Are leadership and no growth compatible?" is rhetorical, for leadership is important to all educational institutions at all times and under all circumstances. The troubles that arise from its absence prove its necessity. Different circumstances obviously require different kinds of administrative leadership. For fifty years, American postsecondary education, like American business, has operated in an expanding market. No growth, however much contemplated in the abstract, comes as a shock to both sectors. The organizational structures and the administrative attitudes and qualities that worked in an atmosphere of expansion will not necessarily be successful in a period of no growth.

At the governmental level, we know that an expanding economy makes it easier to satisfy competing public demands; for example, we can have more guns without sacrificing butter. The crunch comes when the gross national product and public revenues remain level or slide downhill. Then the competition among competing national services becomes really rough. Education is in no way different. The need for additional funds to improve quality and to add desired services is unlimited. In good times additional funds can be found to support biochemical research or a new program for study abroad without curtailing existing programs. A no-growth situation intensifies the competition. Total funding either slows down or actually diminishes whereas the cost of operation continues to increase—not only the inflationary cost of goods and services, but also the legitimate expectations of personnel for increased salaries and wages. If ever leadership were needed, it is in such a situation.

Faculty Reactions

The capacity of colleges and universities to survive, or at least to come through the next two decades relatively unscathed, will depend in no small part on the attitude taken by faculty. Many faculty members, regrettably, tend to make the administration the scapegoat for all their disappointments. Sometimes, equally regrettably, the administration is responsible; but in most cases the president and deans are battling with forces outside their control. The looming decline in the traditional college-age population is not caused by perverse administrators. Although the particularly persuasive state university president may be able to talk the state legislature into increased appropriations, declining state revenues will ultimately affect educational budgets.

The times are hard and will be harder. Nothing is to be gained by cursing the administration and refusing to face the facts of life. If faculties, whether unionized or not, insist on taking an adversarial position, demanding what they consider their just deserts in compensation, tenure, and perquisites without regard for the rest of the institution, the results will be conflict, rancor, and disaster. The more difficult the situation, the more important it becomes to work together and not at cross-purposes.

Many faculties are doing just this—cooperating with results that are greatly encouraging. Recognizing that they are faced with a situation, not a theory, they are sharing responsibility with the administration. This undertaking requires great candor on both sides and great good will. Inasmuch as faculty play a central role in the policies of an institution, their participation in planning for a less affluent future is likely to make the difference between a strong and a weak institution. Administrative leadership must be matched by faculty understanding and leadership.

Trustee Responsibilities

The trustees have an important role as well. Less involved in the daily life of the campus, they often appear to be impersonal and dictatorial. Sometimes, indeed, they are. More often, however, they are deeply concerned for the well-being and survival of the college or university, and their distance from the activities and campus community that make up the life of the institution enables them to take the long view. If enrollments are declining because the college-age group is smaller, if state appropriations are almost certain to decline because of dwindling state resources, then the university must face up to the prospects, however dim. Boards of trustees may have to order budget cuts, but they must do so with full understanding of the consequences. Their leadership will depend on their knowledge of the complex and delicate machine for which they have a major responsibility. Their success will depend on their ability to convince faculty and students as well as alumni and the public that they are concerned, informed, and responsible.

Constructive participation by trustees is important for the success of the president. The job is difficult enough at best; it becomes perilous in times of adversity. The president must carry out the decisions of the board, decisions that he or she may indeed have recommended to the trustees and that need the full authority of the board. When the heat is mounting, the trustees must stand by to support the president. This is no time to leave it to George. Without the board behind him or her, and its full support known, the president's chance of successfully navigating the stormy seas is highly limited. Board leadership is imperative.

Administrative Leadership

There are presidents and deans who thrive in times of prosperity. They dream dreams and see visions and carry their constituencies with them by dint of their enthusiasm. Sloppy administration, expensive mistakes, impatience with details are not important. A stable or declining state requires a different kind of person. At this stage the need is to sort out the educational values which characterize the college or university. Which ones are essential? Which are peripheral and therefore potentially expendable? How important are physical education and intercollegiate sports? Are there academic departments that might be excised in order to strengthen those remaining? Some economies can be effected by across-the-board cuts. These cannot be continued for long without jeopardizing the quality of instruction. Sooner or later the time comes for selective amputation.

What qualities of administrative leadership are necessary for this kind of exercise? The first and foremost is fair-mindedness. The president or dean must be objective and recognized as such. This is no time to play favorites. If faculty positions must be abolished, the faculty must recognize that the president has listened to advice, weighed the pros and cons, and arrived at an honest, objective, and fair decision.

Second in importance is the quality of toughness, the capacity to make the hard decisions. Some persons find this impossible. They will be too easily influenced by the latest argument, or they will be unable to face the prospect of terminating someone's job. It is no fun, but under conditions of no growth it is inevitable.

A third quality is openness and candor. In these difficult circumstances everyone must work together. Faculty cannot be expected to understand and support the president's decisions if they do not know the facts on which they are based. The president must have the capacity to communicate with the campus, to explain the circumstances and the options, to listen to the choices others propose, before making a decision. This sort of openness is desirable under the best of conditions; it is essential in times of stress.

One could elaborate on the qualities of leadership in times of peril, but those three—fairness, toughness, and openness—are the essential core. The problem is how to reallocate the institution's resources. Realignment cannot be accomplished without hurting programs and people. Evidence already shows that it can be done where there is leadership by the president, understanding by the faculty, and intelligent and sensitive support from the board.

3. THE QUALITY OF MORALE— WORRY ABOUT CAMPUS CLIMATE

The Creative Application of Ambiguity in Maintaining Campus Morale

D. BRUCE JOHNSTONE

THE SIGNS OF LOW CAMPUS MORALE are obvious and plentiful. Departments erect trade barriers to hold "their" students. Junior faculty members, as always but now with a special poignance, worry about tenure quotas and their next jobs. Tenured faculty members fear retrenchment and the virtual collapse of mature careers. Researchers lament the seeming conspiracy of fewer funds, more restrictions, and higher overhead. Faculty and staff increasingly perceive an absence of authoritative leadership, but as frequently resent authority when it is exercised.

The faculty may feel burdened by an excessive and overindulged administrative and professional staff. The nonteaching administrators and professionals, on the other hand, may feel overworked, underpaid, and unappreciated by the faculty. Meanwhile, the president faces a diminishing pool of potential students, a skeptical public, a repressively regulatory government, and a hundred faces and voices that seem at times to be searching for ways to feel offended.

Varieties of Campus Morale

Such a recitation of "the college morale problem" may do the topic more mischief than good. In the first place, it is overdrawn by rhetoric. Second, it suggests a set of conditions common to all colleges and universities, when in fact there are enormous differences among the nation's three thousand campuses, including the conditions and problems identified with morale. Third, and most important, a set of examples purporting to illustrate "low morale" perpetuates the concept of "morale" as a unitary, measurable quality with but two dimensions, running from high (good) to low (bad).

In fact, the components of "morale" are complex and disparate. Different persons or groups to which might be attached a common label of "low morale" or "high morale" may differ enormously in the nature, intensity, and cause of the feelings that gave rise to the label. Consider that each

46

individual within any group (any department, school, professional group, professorial rank) might theoretically be measured on each of the following:

- Satisfaction with self, for example, career progress, research productivity
- Satisfaction with the field, satisfaction with one's colleagues
- Liking or respect or both for relevant administrators such as department chair, dean, vice president, president
- Agreement with recent principal decisions regarding the institution, department, or program
- Sense of confidence in the future of one's own department or college
- Satisfaction with one's pay and standard of living
- Satisfaction with amenities, assignments, and other conditions of work

Morale would be unambiguously bad if all members of all departments scored low on all the above dimensions. But it would be difficult to draw meaningful conclusions about institutional morale were some faculty to be very high on some scores and very low on others, or were some to be very high on all scores and others very low on all, or were the most vociferous faculty generally unsatisfied but the great but quiet majority quite satisfied.

One conclusion from this simple observation might be that we ought to perform elaborate "morale assessments" on ourselves, with multiple satisfaction indices, machine-readable score cards, and cells full of data. I hope this possibility does not become fact. I worry about survey research that cloaks our crude paradigms and clumsy instruments with an appearance of validity.

A less ambitious conclusion is that we ought to pay a bit more attention to the particular kinds of good and bad morale and to the patterns, if any, in their occurrences. From such attention, we ought to be better able to isolate the causes— and hence to identify some possible cures—of bad morale of whatever variety.

Morale and Ambiguity

The multidimensionality of campus morale suggests the complexity of the causes of, and solutions to, the generally low morale on our campuses today. Here I shall address one of the most complex factors in campus morale: ambiguity, and its converse, precision or clarity. To many faculty and student members, colleges and universities have become increasingly regimented with rules, regulations, and other trappings of procedure. Faculty generally look uncharitably on the proceduralization of the institution, preferring, if sometimes naïvely, a place where the virtues of creativity, flexibility, spontaneity, and collegiality hold unqualified preeminence over regularity, predictability, and authority. In such a scheme, ambiguity is benign and is to be jealously guarded.

Others, including most outside observers, many administrators, and (for different reasons) many faculty and students, view ambiguity—the absence of clear and accepted policies and procedures—as a principal problem in academic governance and as a significant contributor to low campus morale. Such a view recognizes that colleges and universities, for all the increased administration and paperwork, are still characterized more by ad hoc, judgmental decisions than by-the-book pronouncements. According to this view, ambiguity in college governance is more often than not maleficent, jeopardizing authority, due process, and morale.

Both views, of course, are right. Ambiguity in the proper place and amount can play a vital role in maintaining stability and morale. At the same time and in the same institution, ambiguity that is misplaced can promote suspicion, territorial behavior, and litigiousness. The trick, of course, is to know the difference, and to pursue the reduction of ambiguity when its effects are maleficent and the careful maintenance of ambiguity when its effects are benign.

Maleficent Ambiguity

Ambiguity worsens morale (of whatever variety) when it contributes to apprehension, confusion, delay, or excessively territorial behavior. Ambiguity is generally maleficent when it surrounds procedures, responsibilities, or agenda.

Procedures, or the rules of the game, above all else ought to be unambiguous. How does one get reviewed for tenure? How does a course or program proposal move through the layers of reviews to final approval and implementation? How is a search committee formed, charged, and ultimately disbanded? What steps are required for approval of a grant or contract with a foreign nation? Each of these procedural questions overlays an issue of genuine substance—for example, a decision to award tenure or to approve a program or to accept a contract with a foreign nation. Procedural ambiguity shifts attention from substance to process. The consequences can easily be frustration, contention, impatience—and bad morale—in addition to the diminished likelihood of wise decisions on the substantive issues.

Responsibilities, or who-does-what, ought also to be unambiguous. Probably nowhere outside a college do so many members of an organization, with so seemingly diverse ranks and perspectives, expect—and get—a role in decision making. In the absence of clear assignments, the potential for inadvertently omitting a person from consultation is great, and so consequently is the potential for giving unintended offense. If it is unclear whether or not a particular person should have been consulted or informed on a particular matter, and in fact was not, then the person will almost certainly assume he or she should have been—even if he or she would not have minded had it been made clear before the fact that consultation was not called for. From such small perceived slights grows bad morale.

A third kind of maleficent ambiguity in college governance is that which can surround the agenda of the administration, trustees, or other governing bodies. Surprises are generally bad. Faculty members want to be consulted whenever possible. But they also want, and deserve, to know what the issues are—what is important, and when it will likely come under consideration—whatever their consultative role on the particular matter may be. One of the most appropriate metaphors for low campus morale is "waiting for the next shoe to drop." Often, anxiety about an issue can be reduced merely by making clear when, and under what procedures, that particular issue may move to the top of the agenda of the pertinent committee or administrator. Ambiguity surrounding the agenda encourages the defensive supposition on the part of each faculty member that whatever he or she is most anxious about is probably under active consideration, without his or her views, that very moment. An unambiguous agenda cannot, of course, create either wise decisions or good feelings. But it can reduce what may otherwise be a needless stimulant to bad morale.

Benign Ambiguity

In spite of the examples above, ambiguity is not always constructively reduced or minimized. In fact, a proper measure of ambiguity in some facets of campus governance can be a positive influence in the maintenance of good morale. Ambiguity—again, in proper measure—plays a benign role in the delineation of influence and authority, in the weighting of merit criteria, and in the public assignment of priorities. Let us look briefly at each.

Morale is not well served by the attempt to delineate unambiguously the influence and authority held by, for example, faculties, departments, deans, presidents, and trustees. American colleges have a strong and precious tradition of shared governance. The faculty is in fact overwhelmingly influential in matters of curricular content, in the appointment and promotion of colleagues, in setting standards for admission and certification of students for degrees, and in articulating the general institutional mission. At the same time, the faculty's *authority*—its virtual legal right to decide in spite of administrative or trustee opposition—is minimal. Technically, the powers of most collegial governing organs are strictly advisory upon the president, even though the president acts otherwise at some risk.

The difference between the influence and the authority of the faculty is well known and well accepted. Yet it is rarely codified unambiguously, and the attempt to do so would almost certainly upset the fragile balance between faculty, board, and administration, each of which needs a sense of both influence and authority, but each of which can accept limits that are understood better than those that may be written.

Ambiguity also serves campus morale when it tempers the multiple criteria for merit, whether of faculty members for promotion or of programs for incorporation into the regular curriculum. Probably no faculty member, nor any program, gets truly serious consideration for promotion or incorporation without being "meritorious" by some or by many criteria. But the true task of choice is, unfortunately, less a task of choosing *for*—which is usually easy and pleasant—than of choosing *against* someone or something to make room for the new that one wishes to choose for. At an earlier and less litigious time, a selection against someone or something brought unhappiness, perhaps, or disagreement. But as resources have become scarce, standards tightened, and individuals more willing to defend their interests in court, selections against have become more disruptive, protracted, and expensive. To a degree, this turn is a consequence of our heightened sense of due process and our diminished reverence for institutional authority—both of which are significant and generally healthy phenomena of this decade. Yet our colleges and communities will surely suffer if they become unable ever to select against.

It would be quite possible to accept the propositions of the proceeding paragraph and still draw opposite conclusions about the desirability of reducing all ambiguity in the criteria for selection. It may reasonably be claimed that selection requires exacting attention to criteria, indeed, that the absence of precise criteria for selection invites selection on bases of whim, favoritism, personal prejudice, or other clearly unacceptable grounds. On the other hand, it can be argued with equal or, in my opinion, even greater persuasiveness that multiple criteria are inherently ambiguous, and that our definitions and our judgments and our instruments are not precise enough to reduce selection to a formula that is driven by weighted scores on the several criteria for merit. If the latter view should be more nearly the case, the assignment of scores and weights will add neither to the wisdom nor to the ease of selection, but only to the litigiousness and difficulty of the process. An elaborate set of criteria with scores and weights is unlikely to withstand a serious substantive challenge to a decision to favor a particular program. It may nevertheless give many weapons to those who would discredit a decision for contraction. The foregoing does not imply that academic decisions should be easy, or uncontested, or free from standards of accountability. But the quest for perfect clarity in academic judgments seems doomed to fail, and the failure is likely to leave a trail of contention and delay—and bad morale.

The public assignment of priorities is still another dimension of academic governance where at least a little ambiguity is almost certainly benign. Conventional administrative wisdom often claims otherwise: that a campus or school or department must be able to state its priorities clearly before it is able to make proper academic judgments. This conventional, if simplistic, view has some merit. At the same time, "high priority" like "high morale" can have many different meanings suggesting many different actions. A program or a department deemed "high priority" may be so deemed because it is a jewel to be praised and enhanced, or because it is a mess that needs maximum attention and resources to salvage. Similarly a superb program or department may be in a position of "high priority" to receive yet more resources, or may be judged to be the least needful and thus not in a position of high priority for new resources, precisely because it is in such excellent condition.

In general, high priority programs are programs that need first attention and first resources. They generally get both. Low priority programs are, by definition, candidates for contraction. If they be known publicly to be of low priority, then they will probably lose more faculty and student allegiance, and what began as an unambiguous first position becomes an unambiguously self-fulfilled prophesy. In short, priorities should be studied and discussed broadly and in depth. But the unambiguous public articulation of the high and low priority programs may itself become a major cause for the success or failure of respective programs. If such exacerbation is not intended, then a bit of ambiguity surrounding the public articulation of priorities may be the wiser and fairer course.

International bankers and ministers of finance handle the problem of the self-fulfilling speculation on national currencies very simply: by unabashed lying. The worst thing that can happen to a national currency is to have it known that the currency is thought by its own government to be weak enough to even consider devaluation. Hence, any such consideration must be denied, for the resultant rush to get out of the currency will make devaluation both inevitable and probably excessive. Fortunately, integrity cannot be compromised in college governance, even though clarity can. Honesty and ambiguity thus becomes the compromise, conveying true information, but not enough in itself to turn inquiry, speculation, and discussion into a part of the problem.

In short, ambiguity can serve a benign or useful purpose as well as a maleficent or harmful one. Good morale is served by clarity in certain areas, such as procedures and agenda, and by ambiguity in others. The trick, of course, is to know the difference and to recognize it in time.

Intellectual and Psychic Rewards for Faculty

ADELE SIMMONS

IN ACADEMIC YEAR 1978–79, average salaries expressed in real dollars for all ranks of the American professoriate declined by 3.1 percent from 1977–78 levels. The decline says that salary increases to faculty members at nearly every institution in the country have been outstripped by the consumer price index. The reasons for the decline in faculty economic position are well known, but three need noting. Student enrollments have leveled off after heady growth in the 1960s. The enthusiastic public support that higher education enjoyed in that same decade is ebbing. A large population of Ph.D.'s seek faculty posts—the result of the flood of graduate students in the 1960s and early 1970s who intended to become faculty members and soon created an oversupply.

The decline in faculty salaries may be a result of the convergence of several economic factors in our society—particularly the changing age profile and the weakening position of the dollar. Or, more significantly, it may express deep public disappointment with the institutions of higher education and the teaching profession. Whatever the answer, to the faculty member who is looking for rewarding work, society's lagging support for the teaching profession is demoralizing. While salary levels alone may not determine faculty morale, they are the single most important factor.

Administrators can do so little to increase funds available for faculty salaries that it may seem fruitless to discuss faculty morale. Yet so much depends on good faculty morale that we cannot afford to despair of improving it. Morale among students these days, though constrained by their own economic prospects, is relatively strong. They are, after all, increasingly courted and catered to by our institutions. Administrators and staff of our colleges and universities are scarcely in a better financial position than faculties, but the state of their morale depends on the successful and lively functioning of the institutions. And the institution flourishes only if faculty flourishes.

Inflation, declining enrollments, and public disaffection with higher education, besides holding down salaries, put pressure on colleges and universities to make their programs more efficient, attractive, and effective. These improvements are a matter of urgency for every institution, and for some a matter of survival. Students in the 1960s provided not only the pressure for change but also clear indications about the nature of the programs and practices sought. Today they leave leadership on these matters to others. It is the faculty that must supply the fresh ideas and curricular initiatives to respond to the difficult conditions of the 1980s. But just when imagination and resilience are called for, the faculty feels undervalued and insecure.

In any program to remedy lagging morale, adequate compensation for faculty is a high priority goal and an indispensable element. But what can be done apart from raising salaries? Demoralization is the feeling of being little valued, caught in a situation beyond one's control, and treated without regard for one's special strengths. The remedy must provide faculty members with evidence of their value to the institution, facilitate their intellectual and professional growth, and provide a setting in which the individuality of each person is respected and nourished.

When I came to Hampshire College from Princeton two years ago, a startling discovery was that teaching at an undergraduate institution could be organized so as to increase psychic rewards to faculty while also enriching the experience of students. Hampshire was conceived in the 1950s and planned in the 1960s, its design the product of a golden age in American higher education, when the problem was huge enrollments and the challenge was to spend, not less, but better. Hampshire in its tenth year confronts drastically different conditions, yet many of the innovative practices instituted by its founders appear to foster a relatively robust morale among the faculty. These practices, collectively, seem to reassure faculty that they are valued and to provide them with a setting for intellectual change and growth.

Encouraging Faculty Development

First, from its founding, Hampshire has emphasized collaboration among the disciplines. The value placed on interdisciplinary work is exemplified in the organization of faculty, not in departments, but in four multidisciplinary schools. The faculty evaluation system, which provides for assessment at the time of consideration for reappointment, assures that faculty members will be rewarded not only for professional development as traditionally measured but also for the kind of innovation and often interdisciplinary teaching and research that enliven and enrich the experience of faculty.

Second, faculty and students share responsibility for the design of individualized student programs, and they frequently collaborate in joint research projects.

Third, our close association with neighboring institutions gives the faculty of a small liberal arts college some of the advantages of a large university.

The Hampshire program has the effect of encouraging faculty to explore new fields tangential to or, occasionally, quite distant from their own. For instance, one of the original faculty at his hiring defined himself as a specialist in international relations. Today he is a distinguished author and teacher in the field of human development, specializing in the literature and dynamics of the American family. Another came to Hampshire as a specialist in seventeenth-century French history. She has moved into nineteenth-century American history, with a focus on women and the professions.

In most cases, the new academic interests bring, not a move to another field, but an expansion of specialties. A valued member of our faculty, hired to teach architecture and design, recently submitted, as partial evidence for his evaluation for reappointment, the entire manuscript of his book, just published, on the life of women in rural New England in the nineteenth century. Encouraged by Hampshire's expectation that faculty members will often cross disciplinary boundaries as they grow professionally, this award-winning architect fashioned a distinguished piece of social history from research that another institution might have discouraged— he spent considerable time reading the collected issues of *Household,* a nineteenth-century prototype of *People.*

The majority of courses and tutorials at Hampshire are directed by faculty teams whose members usually come from different subject fields. Through their association in teaching and cooperative guidance of student projects, many faculty members explore new fields. Teamwork also allows faculty members to demonstrate their individual capabilities and per-spectives. Sometimes cross-disciplinary teamwork produces a significant new approach to an intellectual or social problem. For example, a physicist, a painter, a biologist, and a philosopher teach a course that explores the nature of light and color and the relationship among the physics of light, artistic perception, individual psychology, and physiology

Varieties of Stimulus

Probably the most important intellectual catalyst at Hampshire, and a key to the intellectual vitality of the faculty, is the Hampshire student. A curriculum is devised for each student and is the product of consultation between student and a faculty committee. Student interests and enthu-siasms commonly reflect the developing interests of faculty members, with the result that students and faculty frequently collaborate in study projects and occasionally coauthor articles for academic journals. While the benefits to students are evident, faculty members also identify regular, stimulating contact with students as a singular reward at Hampshire.

Our New England Farm Center is an example of the coalescing of faculty and student interests in a research project. Established last year as a demonstration farm, the center is a lively setting for undergraudate in-struction in the natural sciences, economics, and regional studies. In its first project, the objective is to determine whether the small sheep farmer—once vital in the New England economy—can flourish under today's conditions. Students and faculty have undertaken research programs to develop stock, to test indigenous forage crops, and to measure the effec-tiveness of various breeds of sheep-guarding dogs imported from around the world.

Another low-cost boon to faculty morale is our location near the Uni-versity of Massachusetts and Smith, Mount Holyoke, and Amherst Col-leges. As a member of the five-college consortium, Hampshire multiplies by a large factor both its library resources and the number of scholar-colleagues with whom faculty members may consult, teach, and learn.

As Hampshire has developed features that seem to keep life stimulating and satisfying for its faculty, so other institutions may look for ways that are appropriate to their respective cultures and characters. Granted that practices which depart from the orthodox are difficult to introduce into colleges and universities, Hampshire has been able to do so because it is a new institution. Still, education historians have written that even established colleges and universities may become congenial to change, especially under urgent financial need. Perhaps the only good thing to say about today's rough times is that they force us to scrutinize what we do and encourage us to try doing things differently.

Enhancing the intellectual satisfaction of faculty through curricular and organization reforms is no substitute for compensation. Rather, it should be part of the continuing work of any college or university. But when we are virtually incapable of improving monetary rewards to faculty, satisfaction of faculty needs for intellectual stimulation and growth—too often neglected even in prosperous times—merits our best efforts.

4. QUALITY OF ACCREDITATION—
TO MEASURE BY PROCESS OR OUTCOMES?

Process *and* Outcomes

DOROTHY G. PETERSEN

TRADITIONALLY, WHEN ACCREDITING AGENCIES have formulated their standards and procedures for assessment, they relied on the process criterion: the evaluation of such tangible elements as faculty, program, resources, and facilities. Today, interest is increasing in exploring new evaluative criteria and techniques to assess the quality of an institution or program according to its outcomes or results—the total effects on the growth and development of students.

Thus, many consider that accreditation is now at a crossroads and, to improve its effectiveness, must choose between alternatives—to measure by process or by outcomes.

The principle argued here rejects that assumption and proposes instead that the problem be solved by the simple expedient of changing the "or" to "and." The theme then becomes "Quality of Accreditation—To Measure by Process *and* Outcomes." The consequent task is twofold: that of continuing to improve the use of the process criterion while accelerating attempts at evaluation based on evidence of successful outcomes.

Three arguments support this approach. First, despite limitations, the process criterion has worked remarkably well, and voluntary accreditation continues to be a primary force for improving quality in higher education. Furthermore, the accrediting agencies work continuously to strengthen this approach. To consider abandoning it in favor of another approach might cost much of what has been gained in the past several years.

Second, factors such as faculty, library, resources, and others can reasonably be assumed to have a direct influence on the performance of students. Admittedly, research has failed to reveal a direct correlation between a *single* element (such as size of library collection or qualifications of faculty) and student performance. But learning is a complex process that resists efforts to identify a causal relationship between a single component and student growth. Nonetheless, we can assume a direct relationship between a combination of these factors and educational quality.

It is the *combination* of all components which is evaluated by the process criterion and forms the basis for judging the quality of an institution or program.

Third, use of the product criterion, as has been demonstrated repeatedly, presents many problems because it pertains to elements that are difficult to define and more difficult to measure. The difficulties, however, should not deter institutions and accrediting agencies from exploring its possibilities and advantages. Until its methodology and instrumentation have been defined much more clearly than at present, the only reasonable approach is to use both process and outcomes (product) criteria as effectively as possible.

How can the use of the process criterion be improved? Throughout seventy years, accreditation has had its advocates and critics. Criticism has ranged from excessive costs to threats of standardization, but was aimed principally at (1) criteria used by agencies, and (2) methods and procedures of visiting evaluation teams. Criteria have been attacked as being too quantitative, too rigid, and outmoded. Complaints about visiting teams most often concern their composition and competence. What does the record say about each of these points?

Developments in the Process Criterion

During the 1920s, accrediting criteria became steadily more specific and more quantitative. Criticism mounted, and by the early 1930s this trend was halted and, in many instances, completely reversed. A recent study of ninety sets of standards used by fifty-two agencies indicates that most of the regional and many of the specialized agencies, such as the American Library Association, Council on Education for Public Health, National Architectural Accrediting Board, and others rely completely on qualitative standards.[1] Quantified measures remaining in some agency criteria are mostly in the standards dealing with faculty (faculty load, faculty-student ratio, number of full-time faculty, and the like) and the educational program (number of hours of general education and specialization, duration of the program). Of course, several agencies request quantified information in applications, self-studies, and various required reports. The glib criticisms, still heard occasionally, that accrediting criteria specify the "required number of square feet" or "the minimum number

---

1. Dorothy G. Petersen, *Accrediting Standards and Guidelines: A Current Profile* (Washington: Council on Postsecondary Accreditation, 1979).

of volumes in the library" are, however, with one or two exceptions, no longer valid.

Are the standards as inflexible and inhibiting to educational experimentation and innovation as is frequently claimed? Many agencies do prescribe the content of the educational program but most do so for large areas, major emphases, basic curricular principles, or behavioral competences. Few specify courses or fixed curricular patterns that might hamper well-planned experimentation and innovation. Furthermore, many agencies state that they *encourage* curricular flexibility and innovation. The following random excerpts from accrediting standards illustrate the attitude of accrediting agencies today toward educational innovation and flexibility.

> Institutions are encouraged to recognize differences between individual students by providing flexible curriculum plans. (American Dental Association)

> Experimentation and innovation in new teaching strategies and in the design of the curriculum . . . are . . . expected. (American Council for Pharmaceutical Education)

> Each college is encouraged to develop distinctive courses and programs. (American Osteopathy Association)

> NAAB will avoid rigid standards as a basis for accreditation in order to prevent standardization of programs and to support well-planned experimentation. (National Architectural Accrediting Board)

The criticism that agencies rely on outmoded criteria is equally without substance today. Of the ninety sets of standards reviewed in the study previously cited, sixty-six (73 percent) have been revised or adopted within the past six years, and forty-nine (54 percent) have been revised in the past three years. Such figures indicate that accrediting agencies can no longer be faulted for failing to keep their evaluative criteria under continuing review and revision.

In brief, accrediting agencies have improved and refined their criteria in recent years, so that criticisms of the past do not, in most instances, apply. In order to continue improvements, agencies now face the difficult task of attempting to validate their standards.

Until now, accrediting standards have been constructed largely on judgment and tradition about what characterizes a quality institution. Our present climate of accountability is, however, placing strong demands on agencies to base their criteria on solid empirical research rather than on the so-called folklore of higher education. Arbitrary statements found in some standards may shortly be challenged. Accrediting agencies are being called on to justify such requirements as "75 percent of the staff must be employed full-time"; "a faculty-student ratio of 1:10 must be maintained"; "the senior year of the program must be taken in residence at the main campus"; and "regularly scheduled meetings of the faculty should be held." The vulnerability of such requirements lies, not in their quantitativeness or restrictiveness, but in their lack of validation. The onus now lies on the accrediting agencies to collect empirical evidence to justify the requirements. This step is the major task now facing the accrediting community in improvements to its use of the process criterion.

Accreditation Evaluation Teams

Considerable progress has also been made in strengthening evaluation teams and visits. Everything considered, it is surprising, not that the process breaks down in a few instances, but that in general it works so well. Each year, visits involve several thousand participants on hundreds of evaluation teams representing sixty to seventy agencies visiting widely diverse institutions. Moreover, each year sees a high turnover of personnel: according to a recent report, "during the whole period of study [1970–77] about 30 percent of the team members were new to the work that year."[2]

Of special note, all team members are *volunteers* who give generously of their time and service. A recent study of sixty-one agencies indicates that only ten pay a token honorarium to team members or chairpersons or both. The average honorarium is $112 to team members and $276 to chairpersons for the two- to four-day visit, which requires intensive advance preparation plus such follow-up work as writing individual reports and constructing or checking the final report. That highly qualified persons are willing to undertake the demanding task of evaluating an institution or program for little or no financial compensation is, indeed, a credit to them and to the accrediting agencies which supervise and coordinate the enterprise.

One of the strongest efforts by accrediting agencies in recent years has been that of training and upgrading team members. Today, most agencies have refined their procedures for recruiting, selecting, training, and evaluating team members. For instance, of sixty-one agencies, forty-six (75 percent) hold regularly scheduled workshops or seminars for the orientation of new team members. The workshops employ audiovisual aids, role playing, panel discussions, guest presentations, and other devices to train new team members to become competent evaluators. Other devices such

2. H. R. Kells, "The People of Institutional Accreditation," *Journal of Higher Education,* March/April 1979, p. 187.

as team manuals or handbooks are utilized by an even greater number of agencies. Furthermore, forty (66 percent) have built-in systems for evaluating performance by team members so that only the most competent remain in the talent pool.

In short, there is considerable evidence that accrediting agencies have, in recent years, refined their criteria and strengthened their procedures to a commendable degree. Improvement must be continued while, at the same time, they examine the possibilities of increasing the emphasis on evaluation based on the assessment of outcomes.

Outcomes—The Results of the Education

A few years ago, a critic of accreditation said, "One is struck by the absolute refusal of accreditation to look at what is presumably the most important index of quality in a college or university—the students who come out of the place."[3] This critic did not know, or at least did not acknowledge, that accrediting agencies have long been interested in using the product criterion. As a matter of fact, a conference held by the American Council on Education reported:

> There was considerable discussion of the possibility of measuring the product of an institution, namely, the competence of its graduates rather than its more tangible features, such as the number of books in the library, the size of the endowment, and the teaching loads of faculty members. Several agencies described their experiences with measuring devices of this sort. It was agreed that all attempts to evaluate student performance should be studied and the results distributed to the membership of the agencies represented at the conference.[4]

This conference was held forty years ago October 1939. Obviously, the idea of evaluating by outcomes is not new. Obviously, also, product evaluation is not used to any great extent. Why not?

The answer is that few institutions can present to accrediting agencies any substantial evidence about the achievement of their objectives or about the quality of their graduates. As Bowen states,

> At present, institutions know very little about their results and next to nothing about the effects of changes in their procedures and methods on the results. Even much of what passes for evaluation has little contact with true outcomes— that is, what happens to students, whose development is the object of the whole

3. James D. Koerner, "Preserving the Status Quo: Academia's Hidden Cartel," *Change*, March/April 1971, p. 53.

4. *Coordination of Accrediting Activities* (Washington: American Council on Education, 1939), p. 45.

higher educational enterprise. There have been sporadic one-time studies of outcomes in particular institutions and also a number of one-time studies of small samples of institutions, but there have been few systematic ongoing efforts to assess outcomes, and certainly few cases where the study of outcomes has been linked with management.[5]

Accrediting agencies cannot readily structure their policies, criteria, and procedures on the evaluation of outcomes when institutions have difficulty in accumulating evidence of outcomes. The degree of difficulty varies by type and purposes of the program. For instance, the quality of a preprofessional program can be assessed to some extent through follow-up studies of graduates—one instrument for outcome assessment. Consequently, accrediting agencies in teacher education, construction education, engineering, journalism, social work, home economics, allied health, and many others emphasize in their standards the importance of well-documented evidence of graduates' success in further academic study, in careers, in performance on registry or board examinations, and in research. Follow-up studies do produce some evidence of outcomes although they also are limited by using a proximate rather than an ultimate criterion. To apply the latter would require comprehensive, longitudinal studies of alumni plus amounts of time and money that most institutions do not have and most accrediting agencies cannot require.

The problem becomes more complex when attempts are made to evaluate a liberal education. If a liberal education is defined as mastery of a specified body of knowledge, certain incoming, outgoing test batteries can more or less measure achievement. But if a liberal education is defined as the total influence of the college experience on a student, the problem assumes monumental proportions.

Whatever the impediments, progress has been made and more can be realized. The considerable study and activity now going on should provide guidance as institutions and agencies explore the possibilities of assessment by outcomes. A study reporting a pilot project in assessing outcomes in seven institutions provides some guidance.[6]

Accreditation in higher education has made steady progress in its seventy

5. Howard R. Bowen, "Goals, Outcomes, and Academic Evaluation," *Evaluating Education Quality: A Conference Summary* (Washington: Council on Postsecondary Accreditation, 1979), pp. 21–22.

6. Norman Burns, Director, *Evaluation of Institutions of Postsecondary Education: Assessment in Terms of Outcomes through Institutional Self-Study* (Washington: Council on Postsecondary Accreditation, 1978). Conducted by the regional accrediting commissions of higher education; sponsored by COPA.

years and has accelerated improvement in the recent past. Now it must continue to improve its traditional means of evaluation and, at the same time, intensify its efforts to discover newer and better ways of performing the task.

I recently saw a sign in a gas station which parodied the well-known World War II motto of the Seabees: "The difficult we postpone indefinitely, the impossible we ignore." Lest accrediting agencies be accused of adopting this slogan, I suggest that we in the higher education community need to recognize today's challenge and combine our best efforts toward its solution.

Process *or* Outcomes— A False Dichotomy

ROBERT KIRKWOOD

THERE IS GENERAL AGREEMENT that not every aspect of an educational experience can be fully assessed. There is also agreement, less general, that not every aspect of an educational experience should be fully assessed or assessable. Beyond these agreements, there is little concurrence about what "assessing the effectiveness of the educational process" really means in higher education. Some argue that we must measure every aspect of educational experience in order to evolve a balanced plan for the future development of higher education and to provide rational justification for its support. Others believe that every attempt made to measure the outcomes of the educational process will lead to a *reductio ad absurdum* where everything will end up being quantified and the result will be a mere parody of the intellectual principles on which higher education rests.

The uneasiness and even hostility aroused when outcome measurement is discussed in academe parallel reactions to mystical or occult phenomena, perhaps understandably, for, to many, one is as arcane as the other. Higher education has long been a matter of faith, and its practitioners have tended to coast on a number of unwarranted assumptions. Among these is the general belief that certain values are broadly understood, generally accepted, and so inherent in the educational process that they need no further explanation or measurement. That faith and those assumptions have been challenged in recent years, and general acceptance of higher education and its values as sine qua non of American society are under severe stress. Indeed, higher education no longer maintains the priority it once held, and its needs must now be demonstrated in a convincing and persuasive way if it is to receive the kind of support that education deserves in a democracy.

For many, this change may come as a hard pill to swallow because of the cherished belief that education and democracy are inseparable, that without one the other will perish. Although faith in education as an underlying tenet of a democratic society is still widespread, the support for higher education once so readily forthcoming now must be argued against other demands that, in the eyes of some, are at least as important or even more important than education. No longer does education command from the American people their unquestioning support, either moral or economic. There must be better evidence that it is contributing to the well-being of the nation and that it remains one of the fundamental imperatives which sustain a democratic society.

For more than half a century, accreditation has provided assurance that academic institutions were sound and that they were meeting the education needs of the country. Nonetheless, accreditation has been subject to the same pressures of change as all other facets of education. In the early years of accrediting, quantitative measures were the basis for determining the quality and hence the accreditability of educational institutions. If they had so many Ph. D.'s on the faculty, so many books in the library, so many square feet per student, and a few other "so many" things, colleges and universities were accredited. The superficiality of that approach became apparent by the mid 1930s and was abandoned in theory. What followed, however, was no great improvement.

The successor to quantitative measures was process measures, the judgment that if certain processes were in place, good education would result. Among the processes considered essential were careful selection of students (admissions), equally careful appointment and promotion of faculty (appointment and tenure), determination of courses, requirements, and majors (curriculum), and participation of faculty, administrators, and trustees in policy making (governance). Any institution adjudged to be following these and a few other desirable processes (obviously including financial management) was generally determined to be an accreditable institution. But more recent experience and the results of extensive research have demonstrated that process alone is an inadequate basis for justifying the nation's huge investment in higher education or for persuading the public of its value and importance.

Educators must, therefore, find improved means for communicating the value and validity of their endeavors, and the case must be convincing.

One direction in which educational institutions must move is toward ascertaining the effectiveness of the learning programs they conduct. Unfortunately, on most campuses, assessing outcomes has not been tried and found difficult; rather it has been found difficult and seldom tried. A principal deterrent has been the lack of information about how such assessment can be accomplished.

The early efforts to measure outcomes based on quantification tended to reduce all measurement to purely "objective" testing. This practice has understandably been regarded with suspicion and even antagonism by many academics, particularly those in the humanities who hold that in no way can a course in literature or philosophy be satisfactorily subjected to quantifiable measurement. The humanists' rejection of total quantification can be respected; unacceptable, however, is their rejection of all efforts to measure the outcomes of individual and collective student experiences

Guidelines established by the Commission on Higher Education of the Middle States Association for the development of excellence in higher education include some insights into means to measure outcomes without diminishing respect for the intangibles in the educational process. But also emphasized is the necessity for demonstrating more effectively what it is we in higher education are trying to achieve in our colleges and universities. Among the suggestions for approaches to institutional self-study and re-search are the following ideas, which, of course, each institution must adapt to its peculiar needs and particular circumstances.

Approaches to Assessing Outcomes

The deciding factor in assessing an institution is evidence of the extent to which it achieves the objectives it has set for itself. Such evidence is difficult to assemble and to evaluate, but the necessity of seeking it continually is inescapable. The premise is that every institution will engage in a conscientious endeavor to define its educational mission and the objectives pertaining to that mission. Ultimately, three questions need to be asked about a college or univerity: Has it clearly defined objectives that are appropriate to higher education and to its own potential? Does it have the programs and resources to attain them? How well does it achieve them?

The third question is the most difficult, since many objectives hinge on the encouragement of intellectual and personal maturity, qualities that are not amenable to objective measurement or statistical analysis. Neverthe-less, one primary mark of a competent faculty, administration, and gov-erning board is the skill with which they seek answers, criticizing and improving their procedures in the light of their findings. The approaches need be neither elaborate nor solely dependent on mechanical tests, but they should be thorough and persistent.

Tests and measurements are useful, among other means, to discover all that such devices can reveal about student progress in the mastery of subject matter, development of skill, critical thinking, and ability to apply knowledge. A concerned institution tests student achievement both in general and specialized areas of the curriculum, both comprehensive and course-by-course bases, and, when possible, in comparison with student achievement elsewhere. It makes frequent appraisals of the records of its graduates who pursue education beyond the two- or four-year college level. It surveys alumni opinions. It solicits reports from employers. It does not depend wholly on any indices, but searches and weighs them all for evidence of progress or success.

Something can be learned through close observation of student conduct. How responsible and constructive are students in participation in their own governance? What attitudes and maturity of interests do they exhibit in their activities and in their response to cultural, civic, and professional opportunities? Do their interests change while they are in college? What can be discerned about their attitudes toward social values? What are the characteristics of their social life? Do they show increasing interest in scholarship and proficiency as they get deeper into their subjects? Observations of student conduct are of little use in institutional evaluation unless they reveal changing patterns of behavior or growth and at least suggest that the changes are related to the institution's educational program.

A plan for measuring outcomes may well contain these sections: (1) an evaluation of undergraduate scholastic achievement, made by comparing scores on standardized tests with the results on entrance placement examinations; (2) a study of the performance of graduates in senior colleges or in graduate and professional schools; (3) a long-term study of the achievements, both vocational and avocational, of the alumni, based on data gathered periodically and systematically. These latter two steps require continuous cooperation between the alumni and the administration. Intensive studies of classes from entrance through graduation and beyond may be especially fruitful. Optimally, such longitudinal studies are a function of institutional research programs.

Institutional Uses of Outcome Studies

Outcome studies, if they are to be most productive, should accumulate data useful for institutional research and development. Collectively, they are a measure of an institution's sophistication in maximizing the usefulness of the self-study process and recognizing what data are needed for sound planning. They also provide a solid basis for appeals to the alumni and the public for financial support.

Outcomes measurement is regarded by some as appropriate for vocational and professional institutions, but not for liberal arts colleges. The dichotomy thus set up is false because it emphasizes the process of educational experience without holding the results of that process to account ability. Examples of ways that "pure" liberal arts institutions may assess the liberal arts experience effectively and productively are reported for Bryn Mawr College,[1] Princeton (in an analysis of the class of 1952),[2] and Haverford.[3]

Outcome measurement, examined dispassionately, becomes not a threat but an opportunity. It provides means for studying higher education, with results that could enhance the total enterprise and the quality of its achievements. For all the long history of teaching and learning, we know remarkably little about what happens in the classroom, the seminar, the library, or the dormitory. Douglas Heath has provided insights through his studies, but there is much more to learn.

Obviously the process approach to the evaluation of education neither can nor should be discarded, and no useful purpose is served by creating false dichotomies between the process of education and its results. Either-or approaches may be attractive but are also simplistic and fruitless. Process is highly important to the educational experience, and a given process in most instances is designed to produce results. The process must, therefore, be evaluated as a basis for judging outcomes. Some outcomes have no apparent relation to process, and some outcomes appear almost to contradict the intentions of the process. These, also, demand scrutiny.

For the Common Good

Much more study in the entire area of educational process must be done, for we are still relatively unsophisticated in our assessments. Many of the achievements of education are attributed to assumptions that may

1. Ann F. Miller, ed., *A College in Dispersion: Women of Bryn Mawr, 1896–1975* (Boulder, Colo.: Westview Press, 1976).

2. Roy Heath, *Princeton Retrospectives: Twenty-fifth-Year Reflections on a College Education* (Princeton, N.J.: Darwin Press, 1979).

3. Douglas H. Heath, "The Campus as a Learning Environment," *Forum for Liberal Education*, June 1979, pp. 1–4.

or may not be warranted, so that educators must reconsider the assumptions on which we have coasted for so long and which remain a kind of security blanket for many in the academic profession. Although there is need for a certain degree of faith in the educational process, legislators, foundations, and others interested in the support of education are not readily persuaded or convinced by arguments based on faith alone.

We need, then, not only greater attention to outcome measurement but also a concerned effort to demonstrate the limits of what can actually be measured effectively in the educational process. We need more experience in determining what is immeasurable or intangible. If some argue that certain objectives can be set for a course or a curriculum, others will argue that in some way the results can be measured. Still others will agree that objectives can be set but will also accept that we shall always be uncertain about the extent to which outcomes can be determined. Those who, unfortunately, refuse even to discuss the question of outcomes thwart the sound application of basic research principles to their own endeavors.

If we are in a time of public questioning, if we are in a period of self-assessment, and if there is to be a renewal of faith and confidence in higher education, demanding tasks lie ahead. We need to assemble evidence to demonstrate that we have made serious effort to assess the effectiveness of what we do in the name of higher education and to present the outcomes candidly, both the triumphs and the failures. And where that effort has convinced us that certain aspects of educational experience are indeed immeasurable and intangible, we must make that case, too. We must persuade those who are unwilling that unless we undertake to ascertain candidly and comprehensively the results of what we are trying to achieve in higher education, we shall be allowing outsiders to draw overly simple conclusions and thereby permit denigration of its value to the public.

Higher education is in a period when its value is being challenged and its essence and essentiality probed and questioned. It is time, then, for us to do a better job, not dichotomizing the process and the outcomes of the educational opportunities we provide, or the application of research principles which we exercise in our disciplines but refuse to apply to our educative endeavors. There are enormous challenges and exciting opportunities in undertaking a more effective assessment of what we do in higher education. To the extent that we accept those challenges and demonstrate that we are truly as much concerned with the result as we are with the process, to that extent will we deserve the support and confidence of the American people.

5. QUALITY OF PLANNING—
RESOURCE ALLOCATION AND CAMPUS POLITICS

The Politics of Planning

H. R. KELLS

PLANNING AND IMPLEMENTING PLANS in postsecondary institutions in the eighties will encounter practical political and "people" problems quite different from those in the past quarter-century. Despite uncertainties in the economic marketplace and seemingly relentless financial stresses on educational institutions, colleges and universities find themselves pressed to make accurate projections and to arrive at tough decisions about resource reallocation.

This climate, in which the planning and implementing of plans necessarily takes place, affects the very people whom we seek to engage in the processes, often to the disadvantage of the processes themselves. Professional staff members are understandably concerned about their personal and institutional security and become increasingly adversarial in their attitudes. At the administrative levels, external influences and controls remove many leadership and planning options. It is not easy to plan in a politicized, untrusting climate. Even though but few oxes may be gored in a particular process, many persons are understandably reluctant to participate. Unfortunately, these conditions are quite likely to worsen during the eighties, as economic conditions tighten and costs increase.

Unless special steps are taken, planning under such conditions often does not result in action. A twofold question is, What can be done to enhance the effectiveness of the planning, and what procedures can be developed to elicit the optimum participation of the people who will be affected?

Planning has received considerable attention in recent years, with most of the work focused on models and systems of planning.[1] Little attention,

1. *Planning: Universities* (Columbus: Ohio Board of Regents, 1973); S. B. Parekh, *Long-Range Planning* (New Rochelle, N.Y.: Change Magazine Press, 1975); *A College Planning Cycle* (Washington: National Association of College and University Business Officers, 1975); D. Kent Halstead, *Statewide Planning in Higher Education*, U.S. Department of Health, Education, and Welfare (Washington: Government Printing Office, 1979); D. Kent Halstead, *Higher Education Planning: A Bibliographic Handbook*, HEW (Washington: Government Printing Office, 1979).

however, has gone to the human side of the matter—concern for vital initiatives in the psychological and political aspects of planning and resource allocation. Here, higher education seems to drag far behind industry and even some government agencies. A recent review emphasized the nature of participation,[2] and a retrospective study of successful and unsuccessful planning ventures found that the psychological and political dimensions were critical.[3] Lindquist has laid groundwork for much-needed progress, discussed his pioneering work—a readable, valuable book that will help immensely as we negotiate the years ahead.[4] The way we proceed, perhaps more than most of the brilliant solutions our leaders perceive, will bring the answers needed for each institution because staff members must be committed to carry out the solutions.

Agenda for Planning

Some items are obvious. Other useful matters for attention have emerged from the human relations[5] and organization development movements of the last twenty years.[6] A few items seem to me to be especially helpful.

1. We must realize that there is no easy way to plan, to reorder priorities, to reallocate resources, and to change our institutions. Those espousing planning models are naïve if they think that the people at the institutions do not have to create and accept solutions. Those who speak of "creative retrenchment" have probably never lived through one.

2. In the long run there is no substitute for openness, for communication and trust, for treating people fairly, with dignity and with due process, and for involving them as far as possible in various ways in the planning and reallocation processes.

2. Richard C. Richardson, Jr., Roy E. Gardner, and Ann Pierce, "The Need for Institutional Planning," ERIC/Higher Education *Research Currents*, September 1977, pp. 3–6.

3. H. R. Kells, "Academic Planning: An Analysis of Planning Experiences in the Collegiate Setting," *Planning for Higher Education*, October 1977, pp. 2–9 (Society for College and University Planning).

4. Jack Lindquist, *Strategies for Change* (Berkeley, Calif.: Pacific Soundings Press, 1978; available also from Council for the Advancement of Small Colleges, One Dupont Circle, Washington, D.C. 20036).

5. Paul Hershey and Kenneth H. Blanchard, *Management of Organizational Behavior* (Englewood Cliffs, N.J.: Prentice-Hall, 1978); Jack Fordyce and Raymond Weil, *Managing with People* (Reading, Mass.: Addison-Wesley, 1971).

6. Edgar Huse, *Organization Development and Change* (St. Paul, Minn.: West Publishing, 1975).

3. Involvement *can* be creative. Processes can be designed to use people well, and to use intensive, segmented, sequential stages which have a discernible beginning and end. Information can be available when needed. Group leaders can be trained, and problem-solving skills can be taught or enhanced. A host of things can be done to improve *the way* we use people in processes. The gap between personal goals and concerns and those of the institution can be narrowed even under relatively hostile conditions.[7]

4. It is important to build planning capacity over time, and for each institution to build the cycle of study, planning, implementation, and restudy. Study must precede planning and can be so designed that it provides a useful basis for planning and the confidence to proceed with the planning.

5. At the risk of alienating many of the newly acquired academic experts in the law, I submit that some institutions are suffering undue fear of legal action and are unduly burdened thereby. In some instances, advice has been mistaken for mandatory instruction, and the staff lawyer has in effect become a policy setter. Perhaps we are coming to a point where the cost of preventive medicine may be substantially exceeding the cost of enduring the illness. This situation, if allowed to continue, may have deleterious effects on planning and change.

Leadership

Finally, there is the role of leadership for planning and resource decisions in the 1980s. Although a reassertion of the leader role is required, to rely solely on forceful leaders who make tough decisions would be a partial and sometimes harmful solution. The level of stress for our people and our institutions may be too high for autocratic leadership alone. The new leaders must be experienced enough to know what could evolve through a planning process, be talented and believable enough to assist it to evolve, be skilled enough in ways to motivate and involve people in creating and implementing the new order, and be courageous and diligent enough to see the process through under changing and often stressful conditions.

We will have to work harder at creating humane and useful planning and resource allocation processes and at assisting in the development of leaders to make them work.

---

7. H. R. Kells, *Self-Study Processes for Postsecondary Institutions* (Washington: American Council on Education, 1980).

Propositions for the Eighties

ROBERT G. ARNS

MUCH OF AMERICAN HIGHER EDUCATION was still reeling from the turmoil of the late 1960s and uncertain of its worth when in 1973 it was caught by surprise by the second signal that the end had come to its quarter-century golden era: economic stagnation coupled with accelerated inflation followed hard on the Arab oil embargo. The third and final signal is appearing in the enrollment downturn which marks the end of the postwar baby boom.

Nearly all colleges and universities have suffered to some extent from these blows. Most are not fully prepared for the extended decline which is predicted to reach beyond the decade of the eighties. Growth was choked off at a time when some programs were not yet adequately developed and when some others were too comfortable. Meanwhile, the need for change and improvement did not slacken. The knowledge explosion did not die with the golden era; and students continue to shift their interests in new directions at a rate that would be hard to follow in the best of times. The institutions learned to use the annual growth in income to fulfill these needs. Now, waning public confidence, a troubled economy, double-digit inflation, and declining enrollments have robbed us of that tool. Little wonder that some colleges and universities are groping in bewilderment for ways to survive; a pity that only a few are looking beyond mere survival, for ways to respond positively to a changing environment. We in higher education are unaccustomed to putting on a happy demeanor when additional resources are not regularly available.

Baldridge and his coworkers have described characteristics of the political behavior that occurs in universities under conditions of stress.[1] Their hypotheses are now being acted out on campuses across the land. In these circumstances, management and planning must become more technically sophisticated and sensitive.[2] In addition, management of institutions of higher education under steady-state conditions—or in contraction—imposes special requirements that must be taken fully into account.[3] With

1. J. Victor Baldridge, *Power and Conflict in the University* (New York: Wiley & Sons, 1971); J. Victor Baldridge, David V. Curtis, George Ecker, and Gary L. Riley, *Policy Making and Effective Leadership* (San Francisco: Jossey-Bass, 1978).

2. See H. R. Kells, "Academic Planning: An Analysis of Case Experiences in the Collegiate Setting," *Planning for Higher Education*, October 1977, pp. 2–9, and John W. Moore, "Academic Planning in a Political System," Presentation to the Thirteenth Annual Conference of the Society for College and University Planning, Hollywood, Fla., August 1978.

3. Richard M. Cyert, "The Management of Universities of Constant and Decreasing Size," *Public Administration Review*, July/August 1978, pp. 344–49.

these considerations as background, I offer five propositions for planning in the eighties.

1. Since it will take longer to effect change in the absence of growth, patience and perseverance will be essential virtues; ways must be found to establish a firm sense of direction and to stabilize decisions against changes in personnel and fluctuations in the environment.

The first proposition derives from the nature of the change, without new and uncommitted resources, it takes much longer to change; improve, and respond to the environment—far longer than any of us are accustomed to. A danger is that faculty and administrators, seeing the impossibility of immediate substantial change, will not take the steady, small steps needed to reach new goals. The issue is not long-range planning in place of short-range planning, but rather a commitment to *strategic* planning—the establishment of a firm sense of direction to guide both short-range and long-range decisions, the building of a set of hopes and understanding that will sustain the spirits of those who seek a better future.

Given that goals will take longer to achieve under steady-state conditions, a considerable danger is that momentum, once developed through strategic planning, will be lost or deflected by the change of a president, or a dean, or a department chairperson, or a governor, or a legislature. This possibility suggests the need for greater reliance than in the past on the sustaining qualities of the written word and on enduring features of the institution, especially the faculty and, in some institutions, the trustees. Plans must change over time, but they should not be permitted to bounce about at the whim of transient workers in the administration or statehouse.

The durability of a strategic plan and the decisions flowing from it will be enhanced to the extent that the planning process succeeds in accurately discerning trends and in identifying slack resources. Astute planning will serve to protect the institution against buffeting from fluctuations in the external environment and facilitate adjustment to such fluctuations.

2. There will be critical challenges for leadership in finding ways to nurture creative instincts, to tap natural enthusiasm, and to build consensus.

Given the modest pace of constructive change, there is danger that faculty will become preoccupied with survival rather than improvement. The disappearance of the quick fix within institutions has been accompanied by a general decline in faculty mobility and by a decline in travel and other opportunities which have supported the national and international sense of professional community associated with the academic disciplines. With the weakening of external allegiances, which contributed strength to the department as the dominant focus of community within the university,[4] need and occasion arise to build a greater sense of *university* community.[5] The development of lateral relationships which cross departmental boundaries and the development of a sense of participation in a transcendent enterprise should help to bolster spirits. Further, many small institutions have too few faculty members in each department to put together either an effective response to a new problem or a new way of looking at the organization and application of a developing segment of knowledge. For such institutions, the ability to build a critical mass by forging connections between faculty members in different units will be crucial.

In addition to stimulating new relationships among faculty, the leader of the eighties, whether faculty member or administrator, will have to work harder to encourage individual initiative in the face of a natural tendency to turn inward under stress. Fortunately, unless the malaise is of long standing, individual creative instincts and natural enthusiasm are not far beneath the surface and can be brought forth by the sensitive leader. A few words of encouragement, careful attention to process, and a touch of venture capital can yield significant dividends. In order to be successful, the leader of the eighties must not only be technically more sophisticated but, above all, must also have greater concern for the human side of the enterprise, must be able to share authority on issues of principle, and must be able to engage everyone in the search for solutions to institutional problems.[6]

3. More can be accomplished through redirection (turning energies within units to new purposes) than through reallocation (movement of resources from one unit to another).

Most of what goes on in a university is not directly assigned or planned. Faculty members have traditionally had considerable control over their own activities. This latitude has been a significant source of strength,

4. Robert G. Arns and William Poland, "Changing the University through Program Review," *Journal of Higher Education,* May/June 1980, pp. 268–85.

5. Irwin T. Sanders, "The University as a Community," in *The University as an Organization,* ed. James A. Perkins (New York: McGraw-Hill, 1973), pp. 57–78.

6. Michael Maccoby, "Leadership Needs of the 1980's," Presentation at the Third Plenary Session of the 1979 National Conference on Higher Education, American Association for Higher Education, Washington, D.C., April 18, 1979.

especially in scholarly development. As a corollary, effective deployment of faculty time and energy is critically related to esprit de corps. This resource is not subject to administrative control, but under the right conditions it can be influenced by gifted leadership. It can also be squandered.

Under stress, many institutions have turned wholeheartedly to retrenchment and reallocation as a primary tool for dealing with change. Watching to see where next the ax will fall has become a common pastime for many faculty members, at the expense, too often, of their creative development as scholars and teachers. Not only has faculty morale suffered, but also, in these circumstances, department chairpersons and deans have not had the budgetary stability to encourage them to undertake strategic planning or prudent risk taking. If departments are to be responsive and solve some of their own program problems, they need a measure of security sufficient to enable internal trade-offs to be made with safety. Although some reallocation is surely necessary to keep institutions vital, that necessity must be compared with the opportunity to effect change by mobilizing resources *within* budgetary units and weighed against the danger of destroying local initiative in problem solving.

While in a given year a president may be able to reallocate 1 percent of the available educational and general funds among colleges in a university, and each dean might make similar redistributions of up to 1 percent among departments, each department has effective control over a far greater fraction of its own resources. Quite conceivably, 10 percent of a department's energies can be turned to new purposes in a year, though not necessarily easily. But it *is* possible, and an atmosphere of retrenchment and reallocation in the college or university can so distress the academic community as to prevent constructive redirection within the departments and colleges.

4. If the contributions of rationality to decisions are to be sustained, the quality and quantity of information available to participants must be dramatically improved.

Some institutions will unfortunately not have the comparative luxury of being at or near a steady state in their operating resources. Under conditions of contraction, whether due to an absolute decline or to growth rate in revenue significantly below the inflation rate—when there must be retrenchment *without* reallocation, it will be far more difficult to mobilize good will for the benefit of the institution.

The problems of effecting change without new resources and the fragility of the consensus toward constructive change demand close attention to the *way* in which decisions are made. As noted at the outset, circumstances of stress and uncertainty increase the tendency toward political behavior by faculty members and administrators, with the attendant danger that decisions will be based on bargaining rather than reason. Given these conditions, most institutions need a quantum leap in emphasis on process and in the quantity and quality of the information available for decision making.

Some people believe that the power pie is fixed in size and that the challenge is to get a bigger slice at the expense of someone else. Not true. Better processes and improved information can make everyone more powerful. While better information is not a panacea,[7] both administrators and faculty can and should seek to strengthen their positions through information in order to improve decisions. In the past, the emphasis has been on historical information and on input parameters. Strategic planning in a political milieu requires not only better information of that sort but also reliable information about the future, about the changing environment, about outcomes; new ways of looking at costs and benefits, of comparing programs and institutions, and of simulating alternative courses of action. We need to understand ourselves and to see ahead as never before.

5. Because decisions are becoming more complex and difficult, special strategies will be needed to ensure the essential faculty role in planning and governance.

Attention to process is equally important. In recent years many faculty members have had the sense that they are losing power. Formerly it was easy to institute a new series of courses or a new program. Basic assumptions went unquestioned. Constraints seldom played a role. It was not necessary to provide elaborate justification or to make many choices. Now, making the case is much more difficult, and the answer is no more often than yes. The whole thing is time consuming and frustrating. And yet, if we are to succeed in the eighties, the difficulties and preponderant negatives must not become norms. Faculty must be fully involved in decisions and must draw satisfaction from that involvement.

Some say that collegiality has already died. Others say it never existed.

7. John D. Parker and Don E. Gardner, "Information Will Not Make You Well: MIS Reexamined," Presentation to the Eighteenth Annual Forum, Association for Institutional Research, Houston, Texas, May 1978.

But collegial decision processes remain, and it should be possible to strengthen and use these processes to sustain faculty involvement in planning and governance. That involvement must be broader and deeper than ever before, and we must make sure that these processes lead to results—that something happens at the end, and that the something is seen to have a rational basis.

One reason for frustration has been the separation of academic and fiscal aspects of decisions. Often the separation corresponded to a separation between dreams and realities. The faculty proposed—with attention only to academic concerns, and the job of the administration was to attend to issues of implementation. When the faculty members only dream and the administrators deal only with realities, the stage is set for an unproductive relationship and a stalemated institution. At very least, faculty participation in planning and governance must bring together, in resurrected or new collegial processes, attention to both academic and fiscal concerns, to both policies and their implementation, to questions not only of quality but also of pragmatic significance—in short, to both dreams and realities.

Colin Turnbull has described the plight of the Ik, a migratory people of Africa, cut off from the full range of their former territories by the emergency of new national boundaries.[8] The story is grim. As they faced starvation, social conventions fell away one by one. Turnbull reports in graphic terms how the Ik lost all sense of moral responsibility toward each other. It must be remembered that our faculties are being cut off from some of their old territories. They face privation. If the bonds of civility are to be maintained, ways must be found to enrich the internal environment of our institutions so that the faculty will have a sense of hope and of control over their own destinies. Therein lies the ultimate challenge in the decade ahead.

8. *The Mountain People* (New York: Simon & Schuster, 1972).

6. QUALITY OF ACADEMIC PROGRAMS—
MAKING CUTBACKS

Wield the Ax with Courage
and Sensitivity

CAROLYNE K. DAVIS

THE EXPANSION ERA in higher education from the early 1950s until the
late 1970s left many faculties and administrators psychologically unpre-
pared to face a no-growth situation and a concomitant decline in financial
resources. In view of recent budget restrictions and declining enrollments,
colleges and universities are now addressing their economic problems.
Initially most institutions used across-the-board cuts; then came budget
reductions which varied among units; and more recently the actual closing
of some programs has been adopted as a means to protect the academic
integrity of quality programs.

Decision-making processes for program review and possible closure or
cutback can be significantly influenced by the history and style of campus
governance. The development of policy guidelines has been described
elsewhere;[1] here the focus is on reviewing those policies as they affect
students, faculty members, and administrators.

Some disciplines command more power than others. In general, programs identified as potential candidates for closure are low in quality and
usually viewed as less central to the mission of the school or college. They
tend to be disciplines with low prestige and, therefore, low power relative
to other campus units. Once a program has been identified as a potential
unit for closure, a thorough review should be undertaken.

Guidelines to Roles in Program Review

The guidelines at one institution call for an external peer review coupled
with a review by campus colleagues from other units whose backgrounds
appear to contribute to the overall mission of the unit to be reviewed. The
review report when completed is shared with the unit's faculty, which, in

1. Carolyne K. Davis and Edward A. Dougherty, "Guidelines for Program Discontinuance," *Educational Record*, Winter 1979, pp. 68–77.

turn, prepares its written response to the review document. While this procedure is time consuming, it provides adequate involvement of the faculty in the decision-making process.

The initial decision leading to program closure for a school or college is made by the dean and elected faculty representatives who constitute the college's executive committee. The guidelines for program closure review call for the president to recommend a course of action to the regents (governing board) for its final decision. The authority of the regents to make the ultimate decision is unquestioned. However, within the academic units, some aspects of the decision making are subject to much discussion and even some disagreement, for faculty demand a strong role in these matters. University governance structures usually vest the faculty with curriculum decisions, but budgetary matters are usually made the responsibility of administration. Since program reduction affects both curriculum and budgets, the review process should be designed to include consultation with the faculty but retain the final decision authority for the administration.

The role of administration is to see the overall picture of the institution. In making decisions about program or budget reduction, the executive officers must consider how the recommended action will affect the university and the community. Administrators must assure compliance with program review guidelines and negotiate the final solution. Open communications and the education of all constituents are a must in order to defuse emotionalism and maintain objectivity—if possible. Faculty involvement in decision making slows the process, but enhances the credibility of the procedures and serves to dissipate the general mistrust of the administration that is apt to occur during retrenchment reviews.

For the past quarter-century, higher education management has been based on expansion. Now, it is difficult to develop policy guidelines for program closure, but easier to develop them prior to a crisis situation. Events of the last few years have highlighted the necessity to "wield the ax" in order to maintain a viable institution. If an institution has not developed policy guidelines that spell out procedures for budget reduction or program closure, it should do so as soon as possible. Faculty who have been reluctant to face the reality of budget retrenchment and program discontinuance now accept the need for budget reduction guidelines. In fact, almost everyone on campus can agree to the concepts of budget reduction and program closure review. Most people optimistically assume that closure will happen elsewhere in the institution and not to them.

Generating a climate for change and promulgating guidelines prior to a campus crises are facilitated by a nonstressful situation, where immediate action is not necessary to maintain the financial health of the institution. Doherty's recent research has shown that program discontinuance does not provide immediate relief to an institution but rather affords savings over a longer time range.[2] For an institution facing constraints within any one fiscal year, the answer may be selective budget reductions. Here too, faculty and student participation by membership on a budget priorities committee provides a modicum of participation in governance that tends to enhance the credibility of administrative decisions.

Criteria

Each institution must develop its own criteria for program review and budget reduction. Following are the budget reduction criteria used at one institution:

BUDGET REDUCTION CRITERIA

1. Program's centrality to the University, viewed in terms of its pertinence to and support of the growth, preservation, and communication of knowledge

2. Current and projected future societal demands for graduates and/or services of the program

3. Level of student demand for the program (admission to applications ratio; closed courses, enrollment compared to optimum capacity)

4. Extent to which other programs depend upon program in question for services or incorporate it in their own programs; and the relative severity of impairment of services to the University community that would occur if the program were reduced

5. Impact of reductions elsewhere in the University upon the subsequent demands for services of the program

6. Effect of reduction upon the University's relationship with the community, with other universities, and with governments

7. Availability of analogous programs in the community and the relative increase in cost to the student/staff utilizing such outside sources

8. Current reputation and quality of the program—considering national ratings, professional accreditation standards, research productivity, qualifications of entering students, quality of placement of graduates, attrition of students

9. Amount of support program requires from other University resources (staff support, need for space, and other inanimate resources)

2. Edward A. Dougherty (Paper presented at Association of Institutional Research, San Diego, Calif., May 1979).

10. Level of faculty workload and salary level compared to peers; quality of the faculty
11. Financial benefit of program—relative amount of outside funding which it attracts and future projections regarding the availability of outside funding
12. Uniqueness of the program or degree of redundancy of program in terms of other existing programs, degree to which the program could be condensed or combined with another without appreciable deleterious effects
13. Potential expenditure reduction possible relative to overall loss which would be suffered—income, reputation, tuition revenue, etc.
14. Relative ease of future repair of damages to the program
15. Degree to which the program could become self-sufficient

Additional criteria in reviewing for program closure are:

1. Effects of closure on affirmative action goals and commitments (especially if a program has widespread appeal to women and minority groups)
2. Cost per student credit hour
3. Relationship of the cost of the program to other educational needs of the institution as a whole

A major limitation in program and budgetary review for possible program reduction is the lack of an objective data base. Qualitative factors can be interpreted differently by different groups inasmuch as quality indicators are a value judgment. Data analyses are difficult, for the data are presented from at least two different points of view—principally educational and budget—and sometimes hardly identifiable as the same data. Of course, in program review, as elsewhere, data can be manipulated to enhance a point of view. It must also be remembered that an assessment of high quality within one academic institution may be viewed as mediocre in another setting, and interpretation of institutional mission will affect value judgments about program quality. Research-oriented universities undoubtedly emphasize research and publication activities more than does a college that places less emphasis on research

Side Effects of the Review Process

An important matter in program review is the effect the reviews may have on outside funding. Although program review documents are generated for internal decision making, other agencies could demand the reports under the freedom of information guidelines. If a report is critical of a specific program, yet decisions are made to retain that program, public discussion and debate might adversely affect outside funding for the program. Indeed, in some cases, if the decision process is prolonged for whatever reason, the institution may decide deliberately not to apply for a renewal of certain grants or contracts until it determines the final course of action.

Ethically, with any program under a closure review, admissions should be curtailed or, at the least, entering students should be advised about the program's possible termination. Admission decisions are indeed closely tied to budget decisions, and tuition revenue may be needed in order to provide for an orderly phase-out of a program. Admittedly, the grapevine in academia is quite effective, and if an institution chooses to continue admitting students during the review process, applications will drop significantly.

The time line for the decision-making process of review for possible closure will vary from institution to institution according to individual policy guidelines. Because anxiety and stress are engendered by the review, a timely but thorough program review is recommended. Occasionally, the review process is affected by significant changes in personnel. For example, at one institution the vice president for academic affairs left before a program closure review had reached decision. Several months were consumed in educating the new administrator in the review process and allowing him time to assimilate the various data analyses produced during the review. Consequently, the final determination of action was delayed by several months.

Occasionally, a program being reviewed has a high cost, appears to be of only mediocre quality, but is recognized as having a community service value. These programs tend to be in professional disciplines that deliver some type of clinical services to people in the region or state. These programs may indeed have a low campus power base, but if they are of high value to the community and region, they will rapidly gain high community visibility during the review process.

> If this situation occurs, then it may be especially important to consider alternatives to closure such as: merger with another unit or unit within the college, transferring the program to another college within the University, developing a joint program with another institution, or transferring the program to another academic institution.[3]

A review process may be affected by other factors such as press coverage and involvement of the regents prior to the final recommendation. As already noted, a participatory decision-making structure slows the process considerably and thus places stress on faculty and students in the program.

---

3. Davis and Dougherty, "Guidelines for Program Discontinuance," p. 75.

Administrators, too, experience significant stress during a review, for they must spend a great deal of time studying conflicting data reports.

An administrator who is new to program review and closure will be surprised at the enormous amount of time and energy expended in the review and decision-making processes. Time is needed to cope with the many issues and to try to understand faculty and student perceptions. Much of the work will draw attention of the news media, since closure activities generally make "good feature news" for campus and local papers. During one recent review, more than four hundred hours were logged by the office for academic affairs in the closure review process for one program. A second program reviewed took one hundred hours of administrative staff time for scheduled meetings, not counting time used for preparing and studying reports or for replying to telephone calls and the numerous letters received on the matter.

Coping with Faculty and Student Stress

Faculty and students in the late seventies and early eighties may appear more apathetic than in the previous decade, but still their involvement will increase significantly during any crisis. Faculty members who have been noncommunicative and even fragmented into special-interest cliques will become a cohesive unit almost overnight when threatened with possible extinction of their academic home. Once a program has been identified for possible closure, faculty advocacy becomes strong, and some students and faculty members pursue intensive lobbying. Generally speaking, these activities are aimed not only at the administrators but also at the regents. Additional activities may be aimed at eliciting sympathy and support from the public. Administrators must develop strong self-esteem and thick skins to protect their feelings from being injured by "bad press." A president might even be hung in effigy, as has occurred in one instance when an institution announced plans to close a specific unit.

Faculty uncertainty leads to general unrest, not simply among the faculty in the program under review, but in the entire university community. Because rumors rampant can significantly lower morale and because frequent contact with informed leaders is not always possible, a hot line should be established to counteract the rumors. It's time-worthy to delegate an administrator to answer such telephone calls, for it's easier to dispel rumors when they first arise. Providing a quick response is likely to promote a more trusting relationship between the administration and the faculty. A hot line manned by an able administrator helps alleviate the faculty's view that the administration is insulating itself and making decisions without faculty participation and knowledge.

During this period of uncertainty, the institution may lose some of its better faculty members who have become restive. For all those involved in the review process, there will be a definite loss of productivity: less time for research and writing, mental and physical fatigue engendered by the stress situation.

Students in the program cited for possible closure indicate they too suffer stress. Since many of them take courses outside their own department, faculty members in other disciplines may be unaware of their stress and its influence on academic performance. Students' grades may go down because they cannot concentrate on their other courses. In turn, the grade decline feeds the campuswide perception about the quality of the students in the program, and the perception can feed the development of a self-fulfilling prophecy about the quality of the program.

Students, like faculty, perceive program review as a good idea in the abstract. However, once the review has raised questions about the quality of their very own academic program, they, like the faculty, no longer approve of the process. They're apt to find fault with the make-up of the review committee, criticize the data analyses that have led to the conclusions about retrenchment, and actively recruit other students to support their cause. Policy guidelines for program discontinuance should guarantee that a program will be terminated over a reasonable period of time in order to allow students either to complete their degree or to transfer into another program. Students, however, say that once the decision is reached to consider a program for closure, the program is stigmatized. They believe that the program's graduates risk being viewed on the job market as less qualified than graduates of similar programs elsewhere. Needed are follow-up studies of graduates of programs that have been cited for closure, to ascertain the effects of closure on job placement.

Program closure can cause crises to the system and to the persons within the system. Concepts of loss and crisis intervention and of loss related to death and the grieving process, such as Kubler-Ross theories,[4] and Fink's adaptation to crisis[5] form constructive models to handle many of the problems related to closure. Understanding these psychological concepts

4. Elizabeth Kubler-Ross, "What's It Like to Be Dying?" *American Journal of Nursing*, January 1971, pp. 54–61.

5. Stephen Fink, "Crisis and Motivation: A Theoretical Model," *Archives of Physical Medicine and Rehabilitation*, November 1967, pp. 592–97.

will enable an administrator to anticipate certain activities such as those which occur in various stages of grieving. Kubler-Ross identifies these as denial, anger, bargaining, depression, and acceptance, while Fink acknowledges similar stages of crisis as shock, defensive retreat, acknowledgment, and adaptation.

Regardless of whichever theory appears the more applicable, it is clear that program closure provides a threat to the security level of an individual, since he or she can no longer operate in a reasonably predictable environment. According to Maslow's hierarchy of needs, security needs are below the growth needs of an individual for love and affection, self-esteem, and self-actualization. It is therefore reasonable to anticipate that such persons will no longer be able to handle their achievement needs as represented by the pursuit of knowledge (such as research and publication) until their basic security needs have been resolved. Cognitively, persons who are threatened with program closure will have a disruption of their coordinated thinking process.

The rigid thinking and anger at those who are perceived as threatening to their status quo and the initiation of lobbying activities to maintain the status quo are all predictable and necessary behavior patterns. It is impossible to negotiate with faculty at this time, and perhaps the best activity for administration during this period is to try to establish trust and reduce tension by a willingness to listen patiently to other perspectives. Bit by bit these threatened individuals will begin to examine the future. Only at this stage can one assist them in planning for alternatives, even though these alternatives may have been posed previously.

Decisions to close programs will never be popular. They demand courageous administrators who are committed to preserving academic quality in our institutions of higher education. In the best efforts, "the ax can be wielded," gently and with compassion and concern for the effects that such a decision will have on the lives of the many people who are affected by budget reduction and program closure.

Not the Ax, but the Pruning Shears

BARBARA KNOWLES DEBS

THE FIRST AND a most important administrative and institutional decision in program review and quality control is the choice of means for carrying out these vital tasks. The choice must always be made within an institutional and social context, realistically perceived. Some basic questions are: Which instruments, which techniques, are most appropriate here? and Which will be most effective? The answers to these questions must be reached through deliberation rather than expedient reaction to a situation, especially a financial crisis, and, ideally, should be an extension of institutional philosophy and intrinsic to institutional planning.

For small liberal arts colleges, the least appropriate choice of instruments (and of imagery) is the ax. If excision is the ultimate decision, the scalpel is far better. Since the idea presumably is not to kill programs but to help them flourish to ensure the health of the curriculum, the instrument of choice might best be described as the pruning shears.

In one small college, "pruning shears"—as opposed to "ax"—encompasses its set of objectives for the program review as well as some techniques for meeting the objectives. The figure also suggests the philosophy: The academic programs of the college, whether undergraduate and graduate curricula or special programs, are not regarded either as unchanging intellectual abstractions or as visible manifestations of budget sheets. Rather, they should be defined as evolving educational components for which a pattern of growth, change, and decline can be shaped and encouraged. Hence, the pruning shears.

In the small liberal arts college, especially one where there is general agreement about the basic aims and features of the academic programs— the undergraduate majors and graduate degree programs—it is unrealistic to consider closing a program or programs except *in extremis*. That radical step, wielding the ax, would probably kill much more than the closed program. It would in all probability hack to pieces the delicate fabric of trust and commitment on which academic institutions are founded; financially, in most small colleges, the savings achieved would thus be minimal.

Absent the ax, how then to maintain both academic quality and program effectiveness in hard financial times? How also to maintain curricular flexibility and vitality? For small institutions with basically sound curricula and faculty, the most practical answer is constant tending and pruning of all existing basic programs: constant review with an eye not on automatic closure of programs in trouble either academically or financially (the two are not necessarily synonymous), but review with the primary goal of revitalization, reorganization, and redirection. As a corollary, all new programs must be designed and all new hiring done with a view to maximum use of existing resources and long-term flexibility. Prudent programming calls for sensitivity to the potential adaptability of both faculty and curriculum. Indeed, program review and sound academic planning are—or should be—inseparable. Both are essential to the health and vitality of the curriculum and ultimately of the institution.

"The pruning shears" is not meant to suggest that small institutions can or should dodge either the issue or the consequences of program review, on both academic and financial grounds. If anything, the need for quality control is perhaps greater in small institutions than in large because the mistakes are harder to hide. The problem is, How can serious program review be carried out when significant ax-wielding is neither a realistic nor a desirable option?

Program Review in the Small College

As in many other matters in small colleges committed to democratic governance and a collegial spirit, both extensive faculty involvement (preceded by thorough faculty education) and administrative determination are required. In an institution where all significant academic questions are decided by the faculty, it is vital that faculty members understand (easy)— and face (not quite so easy)—the issues involved in serious curricular review. It is vital that they understand that the issues are both educational and financial. Characteristically, in small colleges, faculties are weighted toward the humanities, and a certain abhorrence of all things quantitative may prevail. Therefore, one imperative is that the financial context in which academic decisions of all kinds must today be made be thoroughly and broadly understood. Basic to that understanding is the sharing of full, reliable data: financial analyses of every program must be developed, shared with, and explained to the faculty members involved both in the program itself and in any potential decision concerning it. True program budgets and cost analyses should be prepared for every area (and be as punctilious in the allocation of indirect benefits deriving from each program as in the allocation of indirect costs to it). Quantitative measures should be applied as often as appropriate, and all financial information examined. Departments and programs should know precisely where they stand financially. These activities should be carried out only to provide the *setting* for program decisions, but not to make the decisions themselves.

The final test for whether a program shall continue intact or whether it requires cutting or significant alteration, even expansion, must not be based on quantitative grounds alone. Rather the evaluation of quality, of academic integrity and importance, can realistically be made only in a far more subjective way. Counting how many students from which department get into which select graduate schools is not the answer, although it is probably not irrelevant. What, for instance, is the relation and contribution of each program to the overall curriculum, to the intellectual lives of students and faculty colleagues, to the image and reputation of the college, and so on? None of these factors is precisely measurable. In any program decision, each of these factors and a host of others ought to be entered: the considered judgment—after systematic, detailed review—of all the groups and persons charged with overseeing the college's academic programs, conceivably also the informed opinion of objective outside evaluators, as well as the perhaps less objective but certainly informed representations from the members of the department or program concerned.

Constructive Options

The need to retreat from strictly financial tests for program review is by no means sentimental. Financial strength and academic distinction are not necessarily synonymous (neither, of course, are they mutually incompatible), and woe to the institution that begins to think they are. The real aims and challenges of program review for a small college, in which variations in any direction are especially visible, lie in the attempt to bring some measure of both financial strength and academic distinction to all programs and in the attempt to develop a framework of consensus from which some rule-of-thumb standards, both financial and qualitative, can emerge. With care and patience, both aims can be achieved.

Once both the academic issues and the financial realities are understood, some routine opportunities and actions can be pursued. For example, no faculty member who leaves or retires is automatically replaced. People, departments, program heads have been so sensitized to the need for constant attention to the curriculum—both its quality and flexibility—and the finances, which to some degree it creates, that the focus is no longer on simply academically cloning the departed member or even on protecting the budget line. Rather, a focus has emerged on both specific program-enhancing needs and the more general needs of the institution, including the occasional need to cut in some areas so as to add in others.

Maximum use of the opportunities presented by natural attrition, a serious commitment to faculty development, and discerning and creative hiring are the essential bases for the pruning shears approach. Wielding the ax can kill the whole tree. Selective trimming is meant to encourage new growth from old branches and give new life to the tree.

Evaluation for Action

SHERRY H. PENNEY

HIGHER EDUCATION IN THE 1980s has a unique opportunity to improve its quality or, in the words of the students, to get its act together. Perhaps it is sad that the principal forces pushing in that direction are largely external: enrollments are declining or stabilizing, government support is shifting to programs that aid individual students rather than institutions, and yet, at the same time, government agencies call on institutions to respond to a variety of guidelines and to be accountable in numerous ways. "Accountability" is the "in" word. As one result, institutions have become more competitive, and some have turned to refocusing their missions in an effort to attract new clienteles. These external pressures and institutional responses make assessment of quality crucial in the years ahead.

Articles dealing with university reform often cite the observation that Oxford had a unique talent for making its eighteenth century reforms in the middle of the nineteenth century. The Oxford example is not one to follow: delay is unacceptable. Instead, evaluation which will lead to reform must take place now. If the goal is that all academic programs offered shall be ones of quality, a reallocation of resources may be necessary, particularly if new programs are to be initiated and programs identified as weak are to be strengthened. Only orderly assessment and follow-through will enable institutions to enter the next decades with strength and quality.

Although evaluation is generally recognized as a valuable process, within institutions it is often reluctantly accepted at the very time it is being needed more. Assessment and evaluation are tricky and unpopular matters: both people and institutions typically do not want to be evaluated. One worry about quality assessments is that they are being undertaken for financial reasons with the intent of determining which programs and activities may be weaker or less important than others.

Because learning advances by building on previous knowledge, it appears nothing can be eliminated. For example, if strengthening program offerings on Third World countries is viewed as desirable, should offerings in basic courses in Greek and Roman history be eliminated? Education and research are by nature expansive—witness the bulging libraries and the frustrated librarians who try desperately to find more space while at the same time being told that even more books, newspapers, periodicals, and the like are needed. Yet, if decisions related to new fields have to be made, who better than faculty scholars can help in identifying the new fields and areas within a discipline as well as in defining fields that may be declining in importance. Some areas of scholarly inquiry may become vulnerable; others must be preserved precisely because knowledge builds on the essentials. The problems inherent in this difficult task make faculty cooperation both useful and necessary.

Approaches to Evaluation

Evaluation is not new in higher education, and many approaches have been pursued. Each institution must use the process that suits its needs and current circumstances. In some cases regional and national accrediting agencies act as a catalyst, and the institutional self-studies prepared for them can be quite useful, as can the accreditation team visit itself. If the institution uses the opportunity realistically to appraise its strengths and weaknesses and to identify problem areas, appropriate reforms often follow, especially when the accrediting agencies support the actions. Sometimes, however, the self-study reports are descriptive or play down real concerns lest negative findings jeopardize accreditation.

Similarly, the departmental review by peers or outside experts is a familiar evaluation model, in which the strengths and weaknesses of a single department are stressed. This procedure, however, often does not give emphasis to the department's centrality to the mission of the institution. Limiting the evaluation to individual departments leads to an outmoded method for improving quality, for each department chairman will state, "Provide more money, more laboratory space, more research time for faculty, more library resources, and, of course, this department can be strengthened." Left unclear is what such changes for any given department will mean to the rest of the institution. Will the changes benefit other departments also? And where will the resources be found to provide departments with expanded support?

Self-Evaluation for the Future

Evaluations by outside agencies or external consultants are common in postsecondary education, and these evaluations and on-site reviews should be continued. However, in the years ahead self-evaluation must come to the fore as the most important component of the overall evaluation system. It is self-evaluation that deserves much more attention in order to meet current and future challenges. Self-evaluation is evaluation that is internally generated, responds to an internal need (either to examine quality or to meet financial exigencies), and engages the entire institution. Institutions need to put more of their efforts into internally generated assessment because, in my view, the results will more readily be followed by decisions that will improve the functioning of the organization.[1]

What factors will contribute to the success of self-evaluation? Three areas are important: positive attitudes, comprehensive processes, and decisions leading to action.[2]

If an institution is to proceed successfully with internal review, certain attitudes or climate on the campus will contribute to success. (1) The leadership of the institution should be committed to the undertaking. Self-evaluation cannot be the idea of only a few; it must have the commitment of the leaders in key positions. (2) Receptivity to change is essential. New ideas and practices must be valued rather than feared. Commitment may be evidenced by allocating some funds for new programs and for experimentation as well as by providing funds to evaluate the efforts. In sum, there must be flexibility within the institution, that is, an attitude which says that changing structures and methods will permit better programs. (3) A strong desire for excellence should prevail. Quality in whatever programs or services are offered should be of primary importance. (4) Finally, there must be a high level of motivation to implement the decisions reached. The quality of the decisions and strategies for implementation are the test. If the review appears to have been all talk and no action, frustrations will heighten. To reallocate resources is not easy, but to do so only after careful evaluation is essential.

Self-Evaluation Processes

A process suited to the institution must be developed. In most cases, certain guidelines are useful. The various constituencies on the campus—faculty, students, and administrators—each need to have some role. Appointing more and more committees may not be *the* answer, but developing ways for these various groups to have a voice is necessary. The people on our campuses can and should be effective agents in assessing what is happening and should happen.

1. For information concerning self-assessment, see *A Handbook for Self-Assessment for Colleges and Universities* (Albany: University of the State of New York, 1979); and John Major, "Self-Evaluation of Graduate Programs" (Paper presented to the annual meeting, Council of Graduate Schools, December 1972).

2. See Arthur W. Chickering, "Research for Action" (NIMH Grant # 41780-05) and *Education and Identity* (San Francisco: Jossey-Bass, 1971); also Harold Hodgkinson, Julie Hurst, and Howard Levine, *Improving and Assessing Performance: Evaluation in Higher Education* (Berkeley: University of California, Berkeley, Center for Research and Development in Higher Education, 1975).

The process, once determined, should be known and understood throughout the institution. Moreover, the evaluation of academic programs should be an ongoing process, not something tied to budget reductions or viewed as an exercise to be done once to get it over with.

Self-Evaluation Criteria and Data

With the process outlined, some questions to be asked about all activities being evaluated are essential. A few examples are: (1) What are the strengths and weaknesses of the program? (2) Is the program essential to the functioning of the institution? Would its elimination or contraction create problems within the institution? (3) To what extent is the program, regardless of demand, necessary to an intellectually acceptable presentation of the field? (4) Does the program under review fulfill a unique function within the education community nationwide?[3]

After agreement on the process and the essential questions, a variety of data on class size, enrollments, follow-up studies on students, and academic activities of the faculty need to be assembled.[4] Again, certain questions are useful: What are the faculty's qualifications? What and where do they publish? What types of grants do they obtain? What are the characteristics of the student body? How are these changing? Is any remedial work necessary? What happens to students when they leave the institution? How does the institution compare to similar ones in terms of cost of programs, variety of offerings, plans of graduates, and so forth?

Decisions Leading to Action

At the conclusion of the process, a great deal will have been learned, and now the crucial test is what is done. Successful evaluations begin with combinations of suitable processes and criteria; they end when the research and results of the evaluation are translated into decisions leading to action. If the problems created by financial difficulties indicate that some programs have to be trimmed in order that others can be strengthened, resource reallocation is needed. It will have far-reaching effects on teaching levels, library acquisitions, facilities, and the like. But these implications will have been considered in the review. If an institution does not move from evaluation to action, it will have failed. The decision may be made by the

3. The questions used recently at Yale are found in Memoranda to Department Chairmen from Abraham S. Goldstein, provost (March 26, 1979). See appendix at end of this paper.

4. Many tools exist. See, for example, *Higher Education Outcome Measures Identification Summary* (Boulder, Colo.: National Center for Higher Education Management Systems, 1974); *Institutional Self Study Survey* (Iowa City: American College Testing Program, 1969); *Institutional Functioning Inventory* (Princeton, N.J.: Educational Testing Service, 1968).

committee or committees assigned the task of internal review or by key administrators—the president, the dean, or the provost—who have been informed by the deliberations of these groups. Either approach for decision making should be known throughout the institution. Appeals concerning the decisions may be made, and the designated groups must respond.

By fostering attitudes that are receptive to change, by developing procedures that are known and understood throughout the institution, by agreeing on central questions that need to be asked, a system is in place for evaluating quality that enhances the ability to make decisions. Real location intended to preserve quality can take place. All programs are candidates for the eventual ax, but only some will be cut. Others will be trimmed and may be candidates for refinement or for consolidation. Decisions based on internally generated assessments should improve the functioning of the organization and gain acceptance for decisions reached in order to help the institution prepare for the decades ahead.

APPENDIX
Memoranda for Department Chairmen
Yale University

1. What are the strengths and weaknesses of each teaching and research program—graduate and undergraduate—now offered by you?
2. To what extent is there a demand for each of the programs in your department?
   a) What have enrollment trends over the past five years indicated about student interests?
   b) What shifts, if any, have occurred in numbers of majors or between the undergraduate and graduate levels?
   c) What courses or programs has your department eliminated over the past five years? Added? What have been the results?
   d) What courses remain with consistently low enrollments? Could these be bracketed?
3. To what extent is each program, regardless of demand, necessary to an intellectually acceptable presentation of the field your department represents?
4. Which of these programs would you like to expand? Why and how? Which would you like to reduce? Why and how? Which might be strengthened, expanded, or reduced by consolidation with programs in other departments? Which could be strengthened without a change in their use of resources? How? What programs in other departments or interdisciplinary groups (e.g. the Concilium on International and Area Studies and the Institution for Social and Policy Studies) are an important element of your programs?
5. What new programs would you like to initiate?
6. What priorities among existing and new programs would you establish under each of the following conditions?
   a) if the total resources available to you were increased by 10% and 20%?

    b) if resources were maintained at their current level?
    c) if they decreased by 10% and 20%?

7. If it were necessary to reduce resources, which of the following methods of reallocation and reduction should be used and in what order of preference?
    a) reduce the total number of courses offered without changing the proportions offered at the graduate and undergraduate levels? Which ones?
    b) change the mix of graduate and undergraduate courses and programs?
    c) change the ways in which senior and junior faculty share teaching obligations?
    d) Encourage more efficient use of resources by
        1. requiring a heavy burden of justification for classes less than 10? With what exceptions?
        2. prescribing a teaching load made up of a specified number of "mainline" courses and small classes or seminars?
    e) reduce or eliminate duplication of courses across departmental lines.

8. Should leave policy be planned over a period of years to eliminate unnecessary expense in meeting teaching and administrative obligations?

9. During the next five years, what changes do you anticipate in the make-up of your faculty due to resignations and terminations? Which of the positions to be vacated are the most crucial to fill? Why?

10. What efforts has your department made to cooperate with other departments and schools in reducing overlap in courses and programs, in encouraging new tendencies in the discipline, in making appointments? How successful have these efforts been? What additional efforts should be taken to engage in interdepartmental planning?

11. Should the existing departmental structure be retained at the graduate level, undergraduate level, or both? Should your department become part of a divisional or other group for all or part of your graduate programs?

12. How does your department rank nationally? Has this ranking changed during the past five years? Do you have any reason to expect it to change in the next five years?

13. Are University and department resources (such as library collections, equipment, support staff, secretarial services, space, etc.) adequate to the teaching and research activities of your department? Which are not? Are any unnecessary?

14. In what ways could the resources (personal, physical and fiscal) now allocated to your department be used more efficiently?

A Systems View of Axmanship and Reforestation

WILLIAM F. MASSY

WHEN AXING MUST BE DONE, it should be done systematically—brutal as that sounds—by using orderly method and planning. Although the idea of systems analysis may strike a jarring note in the context of academic planning, no one should want to wield the ax indiscriminantly. Yet, if financial and academic planning is not thought through in an orderly way, the shaping and changing may be or seem to be random and harsh.

The idea of axing or even performing surgery on academic programs has enough negative connotations that we at Stanford have avoided using such analogies. Instead we speak of "vigorous review which may lead to reallocation of resource." We try to focus publicly as well as privately on the fruits of reallocation—new programs in a time of steady-state budgeting, or financial equilibrium within reach in a time of retrenchment. "Reforestation" and "axmanship" are juxtaposed here as a reminder that academic quality depends on creating as well as thinning or clearing.

In approaching systems planning, two points need emphasis. (1) The policy considerations involved in building and using models for long-range financial forecasting must be examined carefully. (2) Certain planning criteria apply generally for evaluating academic programs in an era of scarce resources. As a corollary, zero-base budgeting (ZBB) has its uses for support services but, in my view, is not appropriate to academic programs.

Models for Long-Range Financial Forecasting and Equilibrium

Effective planning depends on having meaningful goals. For academic planning, the achievement of maximum obtainable quality is usually a major goal. Maximum quality, in turn, is translated into specific objectives such as making key faculty appointments, revamping the curriculum or requirements for degrees, or perhaps simply increasing the funding available to certain programs or departments.

Another goal is the maintenance of academic quality over time. Most colleges and universities would find it possible to increase quality in the short run by spending reserves or capital gains from endowment investments, stinting on building maintenance or other support services, and the like. The drawback is that such measures tend to reduce academic quality in the long run. Prudent administrations and governing boards will seek to balance present and future needs, and hence will apply financial constraints that go beyond immediate cash flow considerations. Thus, "living within the institution's financial plan" takes its place as a goal for year-to-year academic planning, along with seeking maximum obtainable quality.

Two mechanisms for aiding the process of setting financial planning goals have been developed and used at Stanford in recent years. They are

(1) an effective financial forecasting methodology; and (2) models for long-run financial equilibrium and trade-off analyses with respect to aggregate planning variables.

Our so-called long-range financial forecast is a five-year look-ahead at the income and expense components of the Stanford operating budget. There are about a dozen line items on each side of the ledger, so the system is small enough to be manageable intellectually yet rich enough to be interesting and useful. Each autumn, growth rates of the income and expense items for each of the next five years are elicited from staff who are "expert" in the given area. (Sometimes faculty experts or outside consultants are consulted as well.) It took us several annual cycles to upgrade the estimation process from mere guesstimating to making considered and unbiased judgments, but that distinction is at the root of effective financial planning. Common sense efforts, if seriously and consistently applied, can have high payoffs.

The forecast is produced on a time-sharing computer, which makes it easy to run sensitivity analyses and, over a period of time, come to understand the effects of both internal and external forces on financial viability. Even more important, however, certain combinations of variables can be linked together by means of computer submodels. For instance, the Stanford model adjusts the projected budget allocation for student financial aid whenever the projected tuition rate is changed.

Long-run financial equilibrium and tradeoff analyses build on the long-range financial forecast. The idea is that the levels of income and expense and certain key policy parameters, such as the payout rate on the endowment and the amount of net program improvement funding to be sought each year, should be set so as to keep the *growth rates* of expense and income approximately in balance. In equilibrium, the economic forces faced by a college or university, together with the momentum of its policies, will tend to keep its budget in balance over time. By analogy, the pilot of a properly trimmed aircraft will have to exert less effort to keep it flying straight and level, even though he or she will have to be continually on the lookout for unexpected changes in conditions.

The model defines the exact conditions for equilibrium and helps the financial planner evaluate proposed configurations of variables—scenarios if you will—against these criteria. The model can also be used to find configurations that meet equilibrium criteria, a process that is called "tradeoff analysis." The academic planner must then decide which of the set of feasible configurations makes the most sense academically, and then translate the resulting aggregative information into projections that have operational meaning for schools and departments.

Considerable literature is available on financial forecasting and equilibrium and tradeoff analyses.[1] The model itself is available to any college or university, at modest cost, from EDUCOM, Inc., Princeton, New Jersey.[2]

Allocation of Resources Among Academic Programs

Financial planning models help provide a discipline to ensure that specified resources can be made available for academic programs now and during the next few years without jeopardizing academic quality in the long run. In my opinion, however, models have not had a very good track record when applied to the evaluation of the cost-effectiveness of individual academic programs.

Perhaps the best known models in the cost-effectiveness category have been developed and marketed by the National Center for Higher Education Management Systems (NCHEMS). Their objective has been to quantify the costs and (in advanced versions) the benefits of individual programs, both to aid internal decision makers and to facilitate comparisons among institutions. Certain goals have been met over the ten years or so that this work has been going forward, but important difficulties remain: (1) The models are so large and demand so much data that the cost of using them is high and intellectual control of inputs is difficult. (2) The models do not deal effectively with faculty scholarship and departmental research, let alone the joint-product interaction of these with instruction. Moreover, the tendency for the outputs of these models to be used uncritically outside

1. The development and use of modeling at Stanford and the models themselves are described in Davis S. P. Hopkins and William F. Massy, *Planning Models for Colleges and Universities* (Stanford, Calif.: Stanford University Press, in press). See also William F. Massy, "Resource Management and Financial Equilibrium," *NACUBO Professional File*, October 1975; William F. Massy, "A Dynamic Equilibrium Model of University Budget Planning," *Management Science*, November 1976, pp. 248–56; David S. P. Hopkins and William F. Massy, "A Model for Planning the Transition to Equilibrium of a University Budget," *Management Science*, July 1977, pp. 1161–68; and Nathan C. Dickmeyer, David S. P. Hopkins, and William F. Massy, "TRADES—A Model for Interactive Financial Planning," *NACUBO Business Officer*, March 1978, pp. 22–27. For an account of a series of experiments that applied the Stanford and similar models to a number of other institutions, see Joe B. Wyatt, James C. Emery, and Carolyn P. Landis, *Financial Planning Models: Concepts and Case Studies in Colleges and Universities* (Princeton, N.J.: EDUCOM, Inc., 1979).

2. The EDUCOM Financial Planning Model is based on research at Stanford by Nathan Dickmeyer, David Hopkins, and the author. It has been developed by EDUCOM into an advanced, user-oriented software product that is being used by more than forty colleges and universities. The work at Stanford and EDUCOM was supported by grants from the Lilly Endowment, Inc.

higher education institutions has been a source of great concern to many commentators as well as university officers and faculties.

Let me offer one principle from economic analysis, or modeling if one prefers, that I think does have applicability to the allocation of resources among academic programs: Planning should try to enhance the strong or promising department or program at the expense of the weak and unpromising one, subject to certain constraints such as goals dealing with the breadth of course offerings needed for general or distributional requirements. Stated this way, the principle may not seem surprising or even worthy of comment. However, it inverts the rules of thumb for resource allocation that work in many (perhaps most) other contexts, and it runs counter to those views of equity that are based on equality of outcome.

For an economist, the fundamental rule of optimal allocation is to move resources from areas of low marginal contribution per unit of scarce resource expended to those with higher value on this measure. (For businesses the "contribution" is usually to profit, but the principle holds for contribution to academic quality as well.) Most situations outside academia exhibit decreasing returns to scale; that is, the marginal contribution tends to decline as more resources are applied, other things being equal. In such cases the applicable generalization is to look for places where resources can be removed from heavily supported units without a significant decrease in contribution at the margin, in order to make them available to units with smaller current contributions where, presumably, there is a larger potential. I have constructed many a management science model for business in which this principle has been a keystone.

But academic quality exhibits increasing returns to scale in many situations. New faculty appointments added to already-strong departments can make a disproportionate contribution to the quality of academic programs. Intellectual synergy often dominates the law of diminishing marginal productivity. Moreover, the idea that programs should have a right in equity to equal access to scarce resources simply contradicts the objective of maximizing academic quality. No institution that seriously aspires to excellence can adopt the equalitarian point of view.

The rule of thumb one should tend to think of first in allocating academic resources is to "feed the strong and squeeze the weak." This is axmanship in its purist form. Obviously, one must also make judgments about what may be potentially strong—for instance, innovative and important—as well as the currently strong, but the principle of thinning and clearing still applies. A mechanism that can systematically elicit candidates for reallocation and then help one to follow through with the resulting tough decisions is a critical factor in the quest for academic quality, even though such decisions may lead to strong resistance on grounds of local self-interest and perceived inequity.

While the above process must depend on local styles and circumstances, it is clear that systematic, high quality, and credible judgments by academic officers such as department chairs, deans, and the provost or academic vice president will form the cornerstone of any successful effort. Credibility is important for acceptance by faculty, and it may be helpful to articulate some basic and easily understood criteria by which these judgments will be made. At Stanford, Provost William F. Miller relied on the following criteria in our Budget Adjustment and Budget Equilibrium Programs, during which the operating budget was reduced by some 15 percent over an eight-year period.

1. Is the program academically important?
2. Is there now and will there continue to be student interests?
3. Can we as an institution be outstanding in this program?
4. Can the program be securely funded?[3]

While these criteria are general, they did provide a measure of credibility and reassurance with respect to academic importance and excellence. They also recognized that Stanford cannot be good at everything, that we should not start (or continue) what we are not likely to be able to do well, and that a sense of reasonable security of funding is necessary for a program to flower.

On the applicability to colleges and universities of the technique called ZBB (zero-base budgeting),[4] ZBB meets the need for a mechanism that can aid the elicitation of candidates for reallocation and organize the process of deciding among them. I have used it with considerable success in the Business and Finance Division at Stanford.[5] However, I do believe ZBB is not at all applicable to academic departments or programs because it

3. William F. Miller, "How Stanford Plans," *Association of Governing Boards of Universities and College Reports*, September-October 1978, pp. 26–30.

4. See Peter A. Pyhrr, *Zero-Base Budgeting* (New York: John Wiley & Sons, 1973) and Paul J. Stonich, *Zero-Base Planning and Budgeting* (Homewood, Ill.: Dow Jones–Irwin, 1977) for descriptions of the technique and case histories of its application in business and government.

5. A brief description of the results is in William F. Massy, "Analytical Techniques in University Management: Their Role and Usefulness" (Paper presented at the annual meeting of the National Association of College and University Business Officers, Atlanta, Ga., June 21, 1979).

runs counter to the nature of intellectual synergy and increasing marginal productivity, discussed earlier.

Academic units must be evaluated holistically, with careful attention to the interactions between subdisciplines and the strengths and weaknesses of particular faculty members. In contrast, ZBB analyzes an organizational unit into components, with each component being evaluated independently. Surely the idea of identifying and ranking options and making decisions that are consistent with funding limits is applicable to academic departments. However, in colleges and universities, the value of the mechanism represented by ZBB is applicable in the support services rather than the academic areas. Other approaches that, while systematic, take account of the dynamics of academic quality and productivity are needed.

7. QUALITY OF INSTITUTIONAL PROCEDURES— THE PLACE OF SELF-REGULATION

Prefer Self-Regulation

ROBERT M. O'NEIL

THIS IS EITHER A VERY GOOD TIME or a very bad time to examine self-regulation in higher education. A trial judge in Pennsylvania had told Wilson College its trustees may not close the doors, and has summarily removed from the governing board the president of a neighboring institution for supposed conflict of interest. Two federal courts of appeals have recently retracted earlier solicitude for the policies and procedures of higher education, with the comment that excessive deference may even have resulted in "abdication of a responsibility entrusted to the courts by Congress." When the issue of a private remedy under title IX reached the Supreme Court last summer, only Justice Powell had anything kind to say about the special needs of higher education. The majority dismissed as "nothing but speculation" the claim that mounting litigation would pose unusual problems for the academic community.

Conditions outside the courts have not been much more encouraging. Although the votes are not yet in, there is a reasonable prospect that the link between accreditation and institutional eligibility for federal funds will be cut by Congress, thus ending a highly visible function of self-regulation. The admirable guidelines on tuition refunds, worked out so carefully by several national higher education groups in response to a clear federal administrative invitation,[1] may be only partially preemptive of a much heavier governmental regulatory hand. To be sure, the final score is not yet in on the last two matters, although the current climate is not encouraging.

Anyone who is as heartily committed to self-regulation as I might well be discouraged. But I urge a second look at the current scene. I suggest, not that self-regulation has been tried and found wanting, but rather that

---

1. "Policy Guidelines for Refund of Student Charges," *Self-Regulation Initiatives: Guidelines for Colleges and Universities*, No. 1 (Washington: American Council on Education, August 1979), 2 pp.

it has not really yet been tried. We in the higher education community have talked a great deal about the values of self-regulation, but most of us have stressed the "keep the wolf away from the door" function more than the broader and more positive aspects which surely transcend the unsympathetic remarks of a Pennsylvania trial judge or even a Supreme Court justice. There are several contexts in which self-regulation may be more or less workable and useful.

First is the setting in which even the most devout proponent of self-regulation would have rather modest hopes. In some areas of government scrutiny—race and sex discrimination being the most obvious—those responsible for enforcement simply do not believe we can be trusted to regulate ourselves. In other sectors, the political pressures for early intervention are so strong that the regulators feel they cannot wait for internal correctives to work. And in still other cases—such as the Veterans Administration and its bizarre notion of what constitutes a full-time student—the regulators understand higher education so poorly that they fail, largely from ignorance, to defer as they might to institutional initiatives.

Despite these lacunae, it seems to me the full potential of self-regulation has not yet been tapped. In many areas of current concern—possible arenas of confrontation between government and higher education—self-regulation is a practical necessity. Requirements dealing with facilities and services for the handicapped, for example, or the compliance of old campus buildings with OSHA standards, could not be directly policed or enforced even with an army of federal inspectors, and a major expansion of the bureaucracy toward that end seems unlikely. Thus the need for self-regulation emerges here quite naturally from the practical limitations on the capacity of government to regulate directly.

In other settings self-regulation offers the most logical response to invitations or suggestions from legislative or administrative sources. The matter of tuition and fee refunds illustrates the constructive relationship between regulators and institutions: The suggestion is that government would prefer to have the job done by the higher education community, even though the statute authorizes direct intervention, with a clear warning that if self-regulation is not prompt, responsive, and effective, the poised sword may still fall.

Whether the governmental hand is stayed by design or by default, the preferability of institutional initiatives should be quite clear. We know the problems, and we have the experience to address them. We can provide on campus tribunals that will be cheaper, faster, and ultimately fairer than any external agency or court. The time and money saved from defending protracted lawsuits or resisting compliance orders can far better be used for the vital needs of the teaching, research, and service for which our institutions exist.

Self-regulation thus becomes as much an imperative as an opportunity. The problems with which we should be dealing—and quite frankly have not addressed soon enough or effectively enough on a voluntary basis— are well known. The recent Carnegie Council report on *Fair Practices* cites some of the most vulnerable areas.[2] The current agenda of the Advisory Committee on Self-Regulation Initiatives of the American Council on Education includes additional and sensitive topics on which it will propose further introspection by the higher education community in the coming months. Clearly, however, such catalysts will be effective only to the extent that people responsible for the role of individual institutions— trustees, administrators, and faculties—believe there is an urgent need to take bolder and stronger initiatives than have yet been taken. If higher education fails to take initiatives in self-regulation, no vacuum will be created, for imposed regulation will fill the void.

Self-Regulation for Social Goals

CHARLES J. PING

IN THE PAST SIX MONTHS I have found myself in a variety of settings discussing the growth of regulation by state and federal government. What is surprising is the common themes in the discussions. The settings have included: (1) A series of meetings of the Inter-University Council in Ohio, an organization of trustees and presidents of the public universities, were largely devoted to countering the move by the legislative fiscal agency staff to refined reporting as a tool of control and thus to move decision making from the campus and the trustees to the centers of political activity and the legislature. (2) A very different setting was a three-day General Motors seminar involving GM executives and engineering and business deans, as well as presidents, from some fifty institutions. The seminar focused directly and indirectly on the role of federal regulations, their economic effects, and the potential of self-regulation as a more effective

---

2. *Fair Practices in Higher Education: Rights and Responsibilities of Students and Their Colleges in a Period of Intensified Competition for Enrollments*, Report of the Carnegie Council on Policy Studies in Higher Education (San Francisco: Jossey-Bass, 1979).

and logical means of achieving the appropriate social goals described by the regulations. The theme echoed the Inter-University Council discussion. (3) A group of business and education leaders were guests of a major coal mining and electricity-generating company in Ohio. We explored the influence of federal regulation on the use of Ohio coal and on the generation and distribution of electricity. One theme was what the company had done, in enlightened self-interest, in the restoration of land that had been strip-mined for coal. These projects were compared with the results achieved by the adverse and at times clumsy hand of regulation.

A speaker at the General Motors seminar suggested that, since regulation is a common concern, we need to reason together to produce what he described as "a philosophy of regulation." The speaker suggested that the growth of regulations (one incredible illustration cited that the reports required on one model change at General Motors, if piled up, would reach as high as the GM building in Detroit) should force reflection on causes, rationale, consequences; in short, the current scene requires the understanding and critique of our regulated society. He further suggested that higher education and business should join in an undertaking to think through and understand the assumptions, reasons, and value of regulation.

At the start of such an examination, I think we need to acknowledge the need for regulation. Thus we are compelled to ask, What are the causes? What are the legitimate reasons for growth in regulation by federal and state governments? As several examples: Would the universities have accepted the imperatives to educational justice without strong affirmative action review and auditing of reports? Would our athletic programs seriously embrace the proposition that the values which accrue to male participants are equally present for female participants? Would we have taken up the task of examining and auditing the use of dollars in research with such zeal without the presence or the threat of regulation?

Three reasons for the growth in regulation of college and university affairs have been identified: (1) a conviction that the institutions, individually and collectively, cannot be trusted to regulate themselves; (2) political pressures for early intervention, as opposed to the slower processes of internal correction; (3) the failure to understand higher education and thus to appreciate the potential for institutional initiatives. There are undoubtedly other reasons. Two possibilities that cannot be ignored are a fundamental disagreement over social goals and resistance disguised as complaints about government regulation.

The issue is not really whether we can live without regulation. Rather than the absence of regulation, the sensible position is whether we can place greater reliance on self-regulation, or regulation by a structure of free market forces, rather than regulation by external agencies, state or federal. Is it possible to defend or justify such a shift, given the legitimate reasons for the imposition of regulations and controls? There are several arguments. One is practical. External regulation requires an external force. The possibility of regulating the many social goals described by law is remote, and the regulations underrate the difficulties and the scale involved. Ultimately all social policy change is self-enforcing. There cannot be enough enforcers; there are, in Mr. O'Neil's words, "practical limitations on the capacity of government to regulate directly."

Another argument used to support self-regulation is its reasonableness in the sense that no one or no group can write universal regulations and still deal with local variances. This truism holds particularly where the range and diversity of the regulated is great, as it is in higher education. Tuition and fee refund is an illustration.

A third argument has to do with return on investment. As for positive change to respond to social goals, greater reliance on self-regulation, it may be said, will, for hours of staff time invested and resources directly applied, produce more change. Or, at the least, self-regulation will not so consume energy that the regulations divert attention from our tasks of serving the goals through research, teaching, and public service.

Finally, in the context of institutional life, self-regulation affects quality. Self-regulation can serve to make the colleges and universities more responsive to legitimate needs of society. It can address the more critical matter of substance rather than mere form, which so often is the only outcome of regulation. Self-regulation, more than response to audits or reporting requirements, can reflect a sense of a public good, of being accountable in matters of just social goals.

The Unfinished Symphony
of Historically Black Institutions

THOMAS M. LAW

THE LEGAL AND MORAL TENETS of desegregation in higher education are generally understood and accepted or tolerated. However, one gray area persists: the lack of uniform interpretation for implementing the tenets. Questions then arise about cost effectiveness and the influences that desegregation is having on campuses and on types of institutions—specifically, the historically black colleges.

The positive, immediate economic effects of desegregation in higher education become apparent from cost analyses of a unified system versus a dual system, which emphasized "separate" more than "equal." No blessing is totally unmixed, and I am convinced that the financial resources distributed to historically black institutions, even under a unitary system, have yet to yield maximum cost benefits. To help understand the reasons, it is appropriate to consider two points in the desegregation process that have been overlooked, inadvertently or by design: the contributions of historically black institutions before desegregation and the expectations afterwards, and the concept of "catch up" financial support.

Most educators today appreciate the tremendous strides made toward institutional parity in our colleges and universities through desegregation; it has opened many doors of opportunity for black students in higher education. Further successes in the coming years might be anticipated as the drive continues for "equality in education," but black educators have come to understand and must continue to heed the warning that "there can be no guarantees." As yet, in our supposedly free and democratic society, we have failed to root out altogether those carriers of our nation's most widespread malady—social and economic oppression. Hardly a black institution in America has not been shaken by these forces of destruction; I am referring to the masters of systematic genocide who remain blind to the educational needs of all of our nation's youth. There are those who,

106

because they cannot see beyond the propaganda and prejudices of their own colorless worlds, would so quickly turn historically black campuses into shopping centers and country clubs.

The Need for the Black Colleges

The future of our black colleges and universities depends upon a general and growing awareness of what these institutions are doing and on an understanding that they are working with, not against, the national grain.[1] It is sometimes hard to understand the reasoning of people who pretend that the black institutions serve no useful mission under desegregation and therefore should be discontinued. It is difficult to comprehend why notable social scientists like Jencks and Riesman view our colleges and universities as no longer being a viable force in American society.[2] Such thinking goes about as far as a bachelor's degree from Howard Johnson's. As they have for decades now, traditionally black institutions of higher learning must continue to be recognized as viable entities in society. But the colleges themselves must be aware that they are battling for survival while pushing forward in the desegregation process.

The predominantly black colleges and universities continue to serve as primary learning centers for both black and white economically underprivileged and socially disadvantaged Americans. Many of their students are now extending the education they otherwise would never have considered possible. This opportunity is something the predominantly white institutions would neither have the desire of providing these students nor commit the resources.

In a discussion underlining the significance of the traditionally black colleges and universities, O. Clayton Johnson has written:

> Of those white "intellects" who advocate closing any predominantly black college, [critical questions] must be asked: Can you integrate the predominantly white colleges next semester, next year, and find space for all students now in predominantly black colleges? And if you can, will you have the programs necessary to fulfill the role now performed by predominantly black colleges in compensatory education and social development?[3]

The black colleges and universities do not fear desegregation, for they have had their doors open to integration for decades. Rather, they fear for

1. John U. Monro, "The Black College Dilemma," *Educational Record*, Spring 1972, p. 132.
2. Christopher Jencks and David Riesman, "The American Negro College," *Harvard Educational Review*, Winter 1967, pp. 3–60.
3. "The Importance of Black Colleges," *Educational Record*, Spring 1971, p. 170.

the loss of educational opportunity for the poor and underprivileged, the loss of jobs and job status, the loss of visible service to the community, and the loss of cultural pride and identity.[4] The development of institutional strength is, therefore, a prerequisite for the survival of black colleges in the next decade. As long as they exist, they will turn out more and more minds trained to see to this country's needs. They will demonstrate to all of society that true democracy in America will be brought about, not by eliminating the black colleges and universities (or any other black institutions), but by recognizing their contributions to society. An additional important point is that equality—instant or otherwise—cannot be achieved unless it is accompanied by catch-up funds to help eliminate the economic blight of these institutions, brought about by benign neglect and the separate but equal doctrine. John U. Monro, in discussing the growing plight of our nation's historically black schools during desegregation, puts into perspective the difficult challenge ahead. "Out of the agony borne too long," he quotes, "out of the duality described memorably by W. E. B. DuBois, pride and courage were emerging, a pride that accepted the past, and a courage to make the future different."[5]

Financial Support Needs

The most immediate problem before black colleges in their struggle for survival is financial strength. There is a tremendous need to upgrade facilities at many of the institutions, in addition to the need for higher faculty salaries and additional aid for students. Attention in these areas is a must in order to retain highly qualified teachers and to attract well-prepared high school graduates. Particularly urgent is the need for funds to develop innovative programs for students who do not respond to conventional instruction and have had poor preparation in high school.[6]

A traditional pattern for uneven support for predominantly black colleges is reflected by their financial struggle over the years. Most of these institutions are small undergraduate colleges, with the majority of their students coming from the most economically deprived segment of the population. In 1974, 68 percent of their freshmen came from families with

4. John Egerton, "Separate but Not Equal: The Public Black Colleges in the South Struggle Against the White Man's Odds," *Chronicle of Higher Education*, May 30, 1972, p. 3.

5. Rudolf Schmerl, "Developing Institutions, North and South," *Michigan Quarterly Review*, January 1968, quoted in Munro, "The Black College Dilemma," p. 137.

6. Ernest Holsendolph, "Black Colleges Are Worth Saving," *Fortune*, October 1971, p. 122.

annual incomes under $10,000. Only 8.5 percent were from families with incomes over $20,000. Most of the black students were financed through loans, scholarships, and governmental programs, whereas white students received the bulk of their support from personal savings, parental contributions, and earnings.[7]

If black colleges are to provide the quality of education necessary in our complex society, they will require disproportionate financial assistance. "All attempts to provide high quality education for seriously disadvantaged youth," says the noted scholar on black colleges, Daniel C. Thompson, "have proven that the essential educational cost per disadvantaged student must be considerably higher than the normal cost per average or advantaged student if comparable achievements are to be attained."[8] Yet the reality has been that black colleges, with the greatest burden, receive the most meager support.

The future for the traditional black colleges can and should be ensured by the public and private policy makers. Additional major support should be derived from the private philanthropy sector. Then and only then can the black community share more fully in financial growth through their own economic growth. The difference between many of the black colleges and the white institutions in institutional achievement and fund raising is as great as the difference in their racial composition. Statistics for the private institutions show endowment per student at black colleges to be less than half that at white colleges. Tuition costs in 1978–79 at private black colleges was only two-thirds that at white four-year colleges. The median expected parental contribution in 1977 for college-bound high school seniors nationally was $1,200, whereas at private black institutions it was $0.[9]

The historically black colleges have never had access to the support shared by other colleges. They have traditionally had little access to the various funding sources, particularly the local community. And because occupational opportunities for most blacks have been limited, few alumni have accumulated wealth.[10] Desegregation is beginning to turn this situation around. Success for the black colleges tomorrow is also contingent

7. Bernard E. Anderson et al., "The State of Black America" (New York, N.Y.: National Urban League, January 1978), p. 72.

8. Thompson, "Voluntary Support to Black College, 1969–70 and 1976–77," Research Report, vol. 3, no. 1 (New York, N.Y.: United Negro College Fund), p. 2.

9. Ibid., p. 2.

10. Vivian W. Henderson, "Unique Problems of Black Colleges," *Liberal Education*, October 1970, p. 376.

on their ability to cultivate "friends" from the business sector and effectively compete for the large grants awarded by major corporations and foundations.

Enrollments

Desegregation efforts have brought some good news to black colleges in recent years: black high school students have made significant progress in gaining access to postsecondary education. Black enrollments in higher education are now over one million, a more than 100 percent gain during this decade.[11] But some bad news will accompany the good. As the doors of equal opportunity opened to black students in certain institutions, those students were walking away from our black colleges, perhaps forever. The black institutions are losing, and will probably continue to lose, a significant percentage of the best potential students. Efforts to offset the losses by gaining proportionate numbers of high-caliber white students have, for the most part, failed. I submit this trend will continue as long as the distribution of financial resources continues to neglect the catch-up principle and hides behind equalization formulas designed for the rich to get richer and the poor to get poorer. Wiggins has observed:

> As desegregation in higher education continues, the privileged Negro student, like his white counterpart, becomes enamoured of privilege and has decreasing feeling for those in his own former estate. Meanwhile, the historically Negro college, in its efforts to help the more disadvantaged Negroes, is in jeopardy— in the ironical name of human rights.[12]

Of blacks enrolled in all colleges, the proportion enrolled in traditionally black colleges declined from 82 percent to 60 percent during the period 1965–70, and from there declined to 43 percent by 1976. So while enrollment in black colleges and universities has increased in each session since 1967 (when the big push for desegregation began), the enrollment of blacks has shown a steady, but slower growth pattern.[13]

The black institutions realize now, more than ever, that they need to become more actively involved in the recruitment business so that they may continue to compete for students with the well-supported, well-endowed white institutions and the community colleges as well. Histori-

11. James R. Mingle, "Black Enrollment in Higher Education: Trends in the Nation and the South" (Atlanta, Ga.: Southern Regional Education Board, 1978), p. 15.

12. Samuel P. Wiggins, "Dilemmas in Desegregation in Higher Education," *Journal of Negro Education*, Fall 1968, p. 128.

13. Mingle, "Black Enrollment in Higher Education," p. 14.

cally, many black colleges, particularly those in the southern states, turned to churches, community organizations, and civil rights groups in their recruitment efforts.

In Virginia, black colleges have failed to develop a strong, effective recruiting campaign in many high schools through their failure to work with mostly white counselors who have been reluctant to let students know about the black colleges, or colleges at all for that matter.[14] I might add that all counselors have a professional and moral obligation to assist all students in their quest for information and guidance about choice of institutions. I hope the day will come when white counselors will point nonblack students toward black colleges and universities. The shift toward universal high school graduation in America will bring even greater emphasis on postsecondary credentials as students enter the job markets, and the need for credentials will help increase the number of "brighter" students black colleges will attract.

Programs and Faculty

Not only must the black colleges and universities mount strong drives to attract students, especially nonblacks, but must also develop strong academic programs to ensure retention through graduation. Black educators have observed that students arriving on campus are eager to learn and willing to work and study hard. However, added flexibility in curricula must be created to meet their needs and generate more options for them. For decades large numbers of teachers and preachers have been prepared; the future need will be for the production of doctors, lawyers, dentists, scientists, politicians, executives, and corporate managers. Black colleges must increase their offerings at the graduate and first professional levels. There is a tremendous shortage of black Ph.D's in this country in certain specialties.

To provide more career opportunities for blacks, the colleges must also encourage cooperative programs with nearby white colleges so that their students may have access to specialized courses. Cost benefits, of course, can be realized if duplication is avoided. I also believe in two-way exchanges with white institutions to permit students to participate in programs in black institutions.

A recent survey of the top administrators in twenty traditionally black colleges and universities nationwide indicates that the quality of higher

14. Peter A. Janssen, "Higher Education and the Black American," *Chronicle of Higher Education*, May 30, 1972, p. 2.

education for blacks has improved. Not only are blacks now attending formerly all-white schools, but also education at the traditionally black institutions has improved. The respondents believe further that the future holds greater promise for blacks who go on to college because, they anticipate, the students will find increased opportunities to pursue vocational and professional training commensurate with their hopes and capabilities.[15]

Another great challenge to our nation's black colleges as a result of further strides in desegregation is the attraction and retention of good faculty. Outstanding black faculty members all too often leave our campuses for opportunities in formerly all-white institutions of higher learning. For some faculty members, to choose to teach in a black college means more than earning a good salary, or advancing in a discipline, or teaching the highly motivated.[16]

An institution's ability to attract good faculty is directly related to its power to draw funds. Conversely, the ability to attract funds determines the capacity to secure good faculty. So what is the motive for teaching at a low salary? To borrow from one of our leading educators, "This is where the action is in American education, and it is exciting and rewarding to work on the most important problem American education faces."[17] It is tragic that teachers with the highest status and greatest amount of experience cannot focus on those students with the least preparation, the greatest need, and susceptibility to influence. Would this not be a positive approach toward achieving educational equality?

On the whole, attitudes of black college faculty members toward desegregation indicate they welcome the addition of white members to their ranks. Concern has, of course, been expressed about whether white teachers are capable of presenting material at a level neither exceeding the black student's ability to comprehend nor beyond his cultural understanding. The need for a teacher to be both an instructor and a learner has been succinctly put by the student who exclaimed, ungrammatically, "There can't nobody teach me who don't know me and won't learn me."[18]

Within the above frame of reference, I conclude that desegregation is an unfinished symphony for the historically black institutions in this coun-

15. Rodney A. Burrows, "Impact of Desegregation on Black Public Colleges and Blacks in Public Higher Education," *Negro Educational Review*, April 1977, p. 68.

16. Dorris Webster Havice, "Learning the Student: A White Teacher in a Black College," *Soundings*, Summer 1969, p. 158.

17. Ibid., p. 160.

18. Ibid., p. 158.

try. Although my analysis of its effects and influences flies in the face of the legal and moral logic, it reflects two economic realities which few policy makers care to address. First, the predominantly black institutions have the need and necessity for catch-up funding based on past, current, and expected levels of productivity. Second, formula funding, particularly in public institutions, is simply a way of saying, Given the same resources, you are now expected to be as productive as those institutions which have a lifelong history of adequate support, although you have a lifelong history of benign neglect.

If this attitude on formal funding continues, we shall never complete a beautiful symphony which would prove to be one of the most cost effective concepts ever developed in this nation.

The traditional black colleges have made long-standing contributions to the advancement of society. As many enter their second hundred years of service, it is evident they will continue their great achievements in education through traditional dignity and self-respect matched with fortitude to accept the challenges of tomorrow.

Cost-Benefit Analyses of Desegregation

JANE BROWNING

WHEN AN INSTITUTION or a group of institutions are moving toward a particular educational goal, the purpose of educational cost-benefit accounting is to identify what is paid (forgone or lost) and what is received (gained or benefited). At this point in the desegregation process, a final educational cost-benefit accounting of the outcome in the public colleges and universities is not yet possible.

In the case of the traditionally black public institutions, educators must attempt an overview of the desegregation developments in an effort to analyze the costs and the gains for equity. Next, the educators must project (as we were not sufficiently able to do in the desegregation of elementary and secondary schools) the future outcomes for each institution and for the institutions as a body.

The results of the research needed to make the analyses of costs and benefits could make a book. The attempt here is to identify "units of costs" in terms of individual activities, processes, services, and changes that are integral to the desegregation process. The categories listed do not imply that the historically black institutions are alike or that the outcomes and costs will be the same for each of the institutions. One further caveat: all costs have their negative and positive aspects, and the various units of costs are usually interrelated—in education as elsewhere.

Among the categories to be examined are accounting for the mission of the institution, the planning process, the students and enrollment, the faculty, the governance structure, the community, and financing, not necessarily in the order listed. These elements are, as noted, integral to all the institutions in their considerations during the rapid, progressive growth of the public postsecondary education system.

Institutional Climate

The desegregation process itself has some far-reaching effects that educators should take into account as they proceed in the research and the cost-benefit analyses. (1) The desegregation process creates stress that disrupts and threatens institutional business as usual—the established methods of administration and instruction. (2) The increased federal intervention has the typical big-government effect of eliminating those institutions that do not fit government-defined criteria. (3) Changes are threatening to the institution's public image and its community status. (4) Reallocation of education resources may or may not result in improvements. (5) The loss of jobs and possibly loss of students might, in the short run, prove to be nothing more than the movement of bodies, a duplication of post-*Brown* v. *Board of Education of Topeka*, which rejected the separate but equal doctrine.

The list continues with several extrainstitutional factors: (6) The mandatory planning process (*Adams* v. *Califano*, dealing with desegregation in state higher education systems) is driven by external guidelines and time constraints that create pitfalls for the planning process itself. (7) It appears that the desegregation process may bring disaster in some areas at the same time it corrects some of the injustices of society. (8) The ultimate good is still questionable. How is quality education to be defined? (9) The process is and will continue to be political in character and value-laden. (10) The powerful growth of coalitions and of monitoring bodies is healthy for the desegregation process.

Research Categories

In preparation for cost-benefit accounting, the needed research and analyses should include the following categories.
A. Mission
   1. The change in mission of the historically black college or university and its significance for the higher education of blacks.

    2. The effects of increased mainstream exposure on the historically black public colleges and universities.

B. Curriculum

    1. The introduction of greater variety in offerings; the disappearance of offerings that have proved beneficial to black students.

    2. The potential loss of the capacity to educate or bring to college-level work those students who lack the traditional preparation for college work.

C. Enrollment

    1. Merged enrollment: Will it be simply two separate campuses? What effects will merging have on faculty and student populations? Demographic data for enrollment planning.

    2. The shift in racial composition and characteristics.

    3. Will merged student bodies enhance desegregation or polarization in the society?

    4. Within academic programs, will enrollments be all black or all-white?

    5. Relationship between test scores and enrollment.

D. Students

    1. Students' need for environments that offer appropriate support systems.

    2. Personal drama and stress.

    3. Adequate and appropriate academic preparation.

E. Faculty

    1. Hiring, firing, and promotion policies.

    2. Tenure rights.

    3. Implication of placement without regard to race.

    4. Personal drama and stress.

F. Governing process

    1. Governing bodies and administrators: their race and educational objectives.

    2. Is the composition of the governing body suited to the needs of the institution?

    3. Are the leaders and managers capable in carrying on the governing process?

The above summary outlines some of the matters and issues on which research is needed for the cost-benefit accounting that is essential for the success of desegregation—equitable higher education for all.

Desegregation Planning for Public Black Colleges and Universities

LEONARD L. HAYNES III

THE MANDATE IN the *Adams* v. *Califano* calls for southern and border states to eliminate the vestiges of racial dualism by desegregating their systems of public higher education in order to meet the requirements of title VI of the 1964 Civil Rights Act. The court's action dispels the notion that America's public colleges are considered full partners in delivering educational services within state systems of higher education. What has existed (and, as the *Adams* plaintiffs pointed out, still exists) is a situation where whites and blacks view public institutions as "ours" and "theirs." Unfortunately, this situation has nurtured the insidious assumption, held by many educational policy makers, that black public institutions are inferior and anachronistic.

During the adjudication of the *Adams* case, the National Association for Equal Opportunity in Higher Education (NAFEO), representing the black college presidents, noted in its *amicus* brief the sterling accomplishments of historically black public colleges.[1] NAFEO notes that, even though public black institutions have operated without the full support of white-controlled state governments and coordinating boards, these institutions have graduated a disproportionately high proportion of the blacks earning baccalaureate degrees, as well as master's and some first professional degrees. Mingle has reported that this record of achievement continues: historically black colleges in 1976 awarded approximately 69 percent of all bachelor's degrees earned by blacks, even though the black institutions had only 43 percent of the black college enrollment.[2]

After considering the brief of NAFEO and other pertinent arguments, the court in the *Adams* case ordered HEW to develop criteria to guide the defaulting states in preparing plans for desegregating their systems of higher education, to meet title VI requirements. HEW's criteria are directed at six states, Arkansas, Florida, Georgia, North Carolina, Oklahoma, and Virginia. These states are required to eliminate the dual system

---

1. See Leonard L. Haynes III, *A Critical Analysis of the Adams Case: A Sourcebook* (Washington: Institute for Services to Education, 1978).

2. James R. Mingle, *Black Enrollment in Higher Education: Trends in the Nation and the South* (Atlanta, Ga.: Southern Regional Education Board, 1979). See also Mary C. Williams, *Profile of Enrollments in the Historically Black Colleges* (Washington: Institute for Services to Education, 1978).

by desegregating student enrollment and desegregating faculty, administrative staff, nonacademic personnel, and governing board in their public systems of higher education.[3] Additionally, the criteria require these states to monitor and evaluate the progress of their planning efforts. HEW's criteria require state desegregation planning to be completed and implemented by 1982–83.

Perhaps the most significant HEW criteria are the historic sections requiring states to strengthen and enhance their traditionally public black colleges in their desegregation planning. Specifically, HEW's criteria require the *Adams* states to ensure that (1) necessary improvements (academic programs, facilities) will be made to permit the historically black institutions to fulfill their defined missions; (2) traditionally black institutions have resources comparable to system white institutions having similar missions; and (3) states eliminate educationally unnecessary program duplication between public black and white institutions in the same service area. The criteria emphasize that any program elimination cannot be imposed at the expense of the black college and that priority consideration be given to public black colleges which are developing and implementing new graduate and professional programs.

Present Status

The desegregation plans in their present form, unfortunately, do not provide a framework in which historically black institutions can reach out to the total citizenry of their states, the country, or the world in comprehensive ways. The protection of turf and historically guaranteed interests have caused state desegregation planning to become highly political. As a result, new program development and implementation strategies designed by state authorities to strengthen and enhance black colleges seldom follow needs-based analyses and manpower directions; rather, they tend to focus on mechanical approaches to improving racial balance while monitoring the status quo.

The desegregation plan submitted by Georgia illustrates the inadequacies of the planning process as it affects black institutions. The attention given to the three black public colleges by Georgia's plan focuses almost entirely on eliminating unnecessary program duplication for the purpose of increasing black enrollments at white institutions. For example, the transfer of education programs by Georgia's Board of Regents from his-

3. The *Adams* case initially also involved Mississippi, Maryland, Louisiana, and Pennsylvania which, because of the *Adams* case, have become involved in separate legal actions.

torically black Savannah State College, a residential institution, to predominantly white Armstrong State College, whose location is considered urban, will no doubt cause large numbers of blacks who traditionally pursue careers in fields of education to enroll at Armstrong. The business programs going to Savannah State may not necessarily attract more white students, as other educational options in business are available at nearby predominantly white Georgia Southern College.

The transfer of programs by Georgia's regents suggests that significant educational outcomes may not be realized; neither will this kind of planning strengthen and enhance the state's historically black colleges. Rather, the regents' response illustrates the state planners' concern to address themselves solely to the "movement of bodies" rather than to the development of a plan designed to meet the educational needs of all citizens.[4]

The "move of bodies" approach at the expense of planning to strengthen and enhance black colleges is illustrated in the plans of the other *Adams* states. For instance, although historically black Florida Agricultural and Mechanical University received new planning authorization for programs in business education and landscape design, the state almost completely emasculated the institution's programs in agriculture and home economics, the heart of its land-grant functions. Thus the action severely limits FAMU's ability to become a comprehensive university.

In Oklahoma high-demand programs earmarked for historically black Langston University resulted in the establishment of an urban branch of that campus in Tulsa. While the Oklahoma plan is innovative, planners paid no attention to helping Langston exploit its land-grant functions toward achieving comprehensive university status.

Limited Institutional Participation

HEW, of course, is not required to demand plans based on predetermined procedures for installing new programs at black institutions. Nor is HEW required to conduct the planning for desegregation itself, though technically its acceptance or rejection of desegregation plans is its interpretation of whether state planning is meeting the criteria. Rather HEW's responsibility under the court order is simply to enforce title VI of the 1964 Civil Rights Act. Thus, there is virtually no guarantee that the federal

4. For an analysis of the Georgia desegregation plan, see Leonard L. Haynes III, ed., *An Analysis of the Arkansas-Georgia Statewide Desegregation Plans* (Washington: Institute for Services to Education, 1979).

government can ensure that desegregation planning will result in black institutions being strengthened and enhanced.

It is hoped, however, that progress can be made toward implementing desegregation, but concern remains over the role of the federal agencies, namely the Office for Civil Rights (now housed in the new Department of Education), in carrying out the mandate of the court. For example, officials in the Office for Civil Rights who are committed to strengthen and enhance black colleges under the *Adams* mandate may not remain in office for the duration of the desegregation process. If political philosophies and national priorities change, as well they may, the likelihood is considerable that persons who lack the commitment required to implement the desegregation mandate would be placed in key policy positions of federal agencies like OCR.

Meanwhile federal officials, particularly those responsible for monitoring and evaluating the planning process, are concerned that further state delays in implementing approved plans will occur because of changes in the national political climate, rather than educational considerations. The delays in obtaining an acceptable plan from North Carolina are an illustration. North Carolina failed to submit an acceptable plan while Califano was HEW Secretary, and after his departure in the summer of 1979, the state's negative attitude toward developing an acceptable plan seemed to stiffen. Most of the stiffening seems to be attributable to actions taken by that state's education officials to prevent what they perceive as an unjust intrusion into matters that only the state can handle. North Carolina's concerns are not unlike the arguments presented by John C. Calhoun during the nullification crisis before the Civil War.

Reactions from black institutions to the decisions pursuant to the desegregation planning process have been mixed. With some exceptions,[5] black institutions in general feel that HEW's desegregation criteria, if followed and fully implemented by the *Adams* states, will constitute a great stride toward achieving parity and equity for blacks in public higher education. However, the black institutions are concerned that education officials in the affected states will use desegregation to cloak efforts to merge or phase these institutions out of existence. In this regard black

---

5. North Carolina has engaged HEW in legal action to prevent HEW from obtaining a desegregation plan from the state. The five black chancellors of North Carolina's public black colleges have sided with North Carolina system officials in opposing the demands for desegregation (see *New York Times*, February 5, 1979).

institutions in the *Adams* states already note that state policy officials have indicated reluctance to commit themselves to plans which require additional financial resources to strengthen and enhance black institutions. The displeasure and uncertainty expressed by state officials and legislatures, coupled with the tentative nature of desegregation planning, many fear, will adversely affect the ability of black institutions to do what they do best—provide access to educational opportunities to black Americans.

The greatest concern expressed by black public institutions in the *Adams* states has been their lack of input to the shape of the planning process. Without exception, black institutions report that desegregation planning makes no attempt to articulate the concerns and problems of black public institutions as perceived by the institutions themselves. The absence of black institutional contribution can probably be attributed to several factors: (1) the limited involvement these institutions have in state educational decision making, (2) growing misgivings by black institutions about operating within a planning framework over which they have virtually no control, and (3) in some cases, simply the lack of institutional initiative in demanding full participation in desegregation planning.

Need for Better Planning

There are ways of developing and implementing comprehensive desegregation planning that solicit meaningful, constructive input from black institutions. For instance, education officials at the state and institutional levels should make more use of (1) industry-occupation matrices drawn up by local departments, (2) occupational projections, derived in cooperation with other appropriate agencies, (3) occupational and personal needs analyses prepared for planning purposes, and (4) demographic and economic studies, to be correlated with present and future conditions. These invaluable data resources would contribute to rational academic decision making in the development of institutional missions and roles, enabling the state to prepare better plans for its population over age sixteen as well as respond to the desegregation mandate. Needs analyses of these kinds conducted as a planning backdrop would be especially beneficial to black colleges seeking enhancement and strength in the desegregation process.

As the states and their public institutions develop comprehensive needs assessments, several courses of action constructive to the black colleges should emerge.

The states would provide for black colleges to initiate postbaccalaureate programs that focus on societal problem solving, urban administration, health-related problems, and human resource development. With post-baccalaureate programs, the historically black public colleges will be strengthened; without them, growth and ultimate social and economic value will remain limited and access to research and public service dollars cut off.

The black colleges' capacity for public service functions should be enhanced under successful implementation of the desegregation process according to HEW's criteria. The black public colleges in general have been denied the opportunity by their states to serve all citizens. The land grant institutions have come closest even though their programs have been limited to extension activities principally for disadvantaged groups. The public service function in higher education, when appropriately defined, includes applied research and technical assistance carried on for a variety of state and local agencies. State support to increase the public service function plays a special role in the enhancement of black colleges because the types and extent of public service constitute a critical measure in assessing the social and economic utility of institutions.

However state planners construct increased and expanded roles for black institutions in the system, white institutions are not thereby relieved of responsibility to provide access to blacks and other minorities. Rather, they must be held accountable as public institutions to deliver educational services to meet the needs of all citizens.

States must also consider means to upgrade cognitive and effective outcomes for students who are classified as socioeconomically disadvantaged, regardless of whether they attend black or white institutions. State plans need to include mandates for procedures in instruction management to ensure that remediation and development programs are in place and appropriate to their purpose. In this matter—and crucial—neither whites nor blacks should regard the black colleges as that part of the system where academic remediation and reclamation takes place. The joint responsibility of black and white institutions for remediation and development programs must be integral to the rigorous needs analysis conducted for comprehensive, long-range academic planning. The issues of roles and responsibilities of all institutions in the system must be addressed if the intended outcomes of the desegregation process are to be realized.

In the desegregation planning process, one dimension that demands attention is the black colleges' perception of their role in the delivery of educational services. A problem to be faced is the extent to which the desegregation process redefines the role and scope that black colleges are to occupy in desegregated systems. In this context, black colleges will have to chart a development that counters their efforts to be all things to all constituencies. The black institutions can pursue this course by becoming highly selective in programs to be emphasized, by deciding what they can do best and expending their energies and resources for those purposes. In so doing, they will be able to narrow the base of their operations but strengthen and extend the programs selected.

Prospects

Although HEW's desegregation criteria insist that states adhere to goals and timetables, a reasonable assumption is that the desegregation process will take longer to complete than the five years initially established by the court in the *Adams* case. The complexity of higher education and uncertainty about political, financial, legal, and moral commitments to higher education suggest that desegregation in higher education will not be conducted with "all deliberate speed." Nevertheless, the *Adams* mandate provides, for the first time in history, a blueprint for eliminating the dual system and for providing more and better educational opportunities for blacks and other minorities.

APPENDIX

HISTORICALLY BLACK PUBLIC FOUR-YEAR COLLEGES
IN SIX *Adams* STATES

Institution	*Year Founded*
*1. University of Arkansas at Pine Bluff Pine Bluff, Arkansas	1873
"2. Florida A&M University Tallahassee, Florida	1887
3. Albany State College Albany, Georgia	1903
*4. Fort Valley State College Fort Valley, Georgia	1895
5. Savannah State College Savannah, Georgia	1891
6. Elizabeth City State University Elizabeth City, North Carolina	1891
7. Fayetteville State University Fayetteville, North Carolina	1887
"8. North Carolina A&T University Greensboro, North Carolina	1891
9. North Carolina Central University Durham, North Carolina	1910
10. Winston-Salem State University Winston-Salem, North Carolina	1892
*11. Langston University Langston, Oklahoma	1897
12. Norfolk State University Norfolk, Virginia	1882
"13. Virginia State University Petersburg, Virginia	1882

*Land-grant college.

American Council on Education

The American Council on Education, founded in 1918 and composed of institutions of higher education and national and regional education associations, is the nation's major nongovernmental coordinating body for postsecondary education. Through voluntary and cooperative action, the Council provides comprehensive leadership for improving educational standards, policies, procedures, and services.